C000082031

Ultimate Diabetic Cookbook for Beginners

1800+ Days of Simple, Delicious, Low-Sugar & Low-Carb Recipes. Perfect Diet for Prediabetes & Type 2 Diabetes. Includes 30-Day Meal Plan

Amanda Ray

© Copyright 2023 - All rights reserved.

The content contained within this book may not be reproduced, duplicated, or transmitted without direct written permission from the author or the publisher.

Under no circumstances will any blame or legal responsibility be held against the publisher, or author, for any damages, reparation, or monetary loss due to the information contained within this book, either directly or indirectly.

<u>Legal Notice:</u>

This book is copyright protected. It is only for personal use. You cannot amend, distribute, sell, use, quote, or paraphrase any part, or the content within this book, without the consent of the author or publisher.

<u>Disclaimer Notice:</u>

Please note the information contained within this document is for educational and entertainment purposes only. All effort has been executed to present accurate, up-to-date, reliable, and complete information. No warranties of any kind are declared or implied. Readers acknowledge that the author is not engaged in the rendering of legal, financial, medical, or professional advice. The content within this book has been derived from various sources. Please consult with a qualified healthcare provider before making any changes in your diet or lifestyle.

By reading this document, the reader agrees that under no circumstances is the author responsible for any losses, direct or indirect, that are incurred as a result of the use of the information contained within this document, including, but not limited to, errors, omissions, or inaccuracies.

Table of Content

Introduction

Welcome to the «Diabetic Cookbook for Beginners». Tailored for those with Type 2 diabetes, this guide also offers options for individuals managing Type 1 diabetes. We recognize both types' distinct challenges and dietary requirements and have meticulously curated recipes suitable for everyone.

Whether you've been recently diagnosed, have been navigating the intricacies of diabetes for a while, or are searching for a more health-conscious lifestyle, this cookbook is crafted especially for you.

Diabetes, a global health concern affecting millions, mandates a holistic strategy for effective management. Diet is undeniably a crucial element in this strategy. Our dietary decisions can significantly impact our general health and blood sugar levels. Contrary to popular belief, a diabetic-friendly diet is not synonymous with flavorless, monotonous meals. Instead, it's an opportunity to embrace an array of flavors, foods, and cooking styles, all while ensuring they're conducive to your health requirements.

Here's what you can expect in this cookbook:

- Simple, Wholesome Recipes: These beginner-friendly recipes don't compromise on taste. From breakfast to dinner, we've got your meals sorted.

- Nutritional Information: Each recipe is accompanied by detailed nutritional facts, assisting you in making informed dietary decisions.

- Diverse Cuisine: Dive into an assortment of globally-inspired dishes, all modified to be diabetic-friendly, ensuring your meal plans remain exciting and varied.

- Tips and Tricks: Benefit from insights on ingredient substitutions, meal prepping, and other essentials that make your culinary experience enjoyable and mindful of health needs.

Remember, embracing a diabetic diet isn't about restrictions. It's about opting for foods that nourish, stabilize blood sugar levels, and satisfy your culinary cravings. As you venture into mindful eating, be assured that every choice geared towards health is a positive stride towards enhanced well-being and vitality.

Thank you for selecting this cookbook as your trusted kitchen ally. Let's explore, relish, and acknowledge the transformative power of nutritious and delicious food.

Cheers to delightful dishes and a journey towards better health. Bon Appétit!

Chapter 1: Diabetic Diet

What is Diabetes?

A medical disorder called diabetes affects how your body uses glucose, a type of sugar in your blood.

Usually, our body breaks down food into tiny pieces when we eat. One of these pieces is glucose, which our cells use for energy. To help glucose enter our cells, our pancreas makes a hormone called insulin. Think of insulin as a key that opens doors to our cells, letting the glucose in.

But with diabetes, something goes wrong with this system.

Either:

- The pancreas doesn't make enough insulin.
- Or the body can't use the insulin it produces correctly.

Because of this, the glucose stays in our blood instead of feeding our cells, leading to higher blood sugar levels. Over time, having too much sugar in your blood can cause health problems.

That's why what we eat is so important. The proper diet can support stable blood sugar levels. This cookbook will guide you through choosing and preparing tasty and good foods for managing diabetes.

Types of Diabetes

Before we delve into the world of delicious recipes tailored for those managing diabetes, it's crucial to understand the condition in its various forms. Just as no two people are entirely alike, diabetes also presents itself differently among individuals. Diabetes can be categorized into three primary types, each with its unique causes and management approaches. By recognizing and understanding these distinctions, you'll be better equipped to navigate the culinary choices that best suit your health needs.

Let's take a closer look at these types.

Type 1 Diabetes

Imagine your body as a factory. Within this factory, there's a dedicated team responsible for producing special «keys» known as insulin. Because they let sugar into your cells, these keys give them the energy required to function. However, in

Type 1 diabetes, something goes awry. The body's defense system mistakenly recognizes this team as a threat and launches an attack, destroying them. As a result, the body stops producing its insulin. Hence, individuals with Type 1 diabetes must rely on external sources, such as injections or pumps, to supply the insulin their body requires to utilize the sugar from their food.

Dietary Guidelines for Type 1 Diabetes

Carbohydrate Counting: For those with Type 1 diabetes, insulin is administered based on carbohydrate intake. Hence, developing an understanding and skill in accurately counting carbohydrates becomes paramount. Doing so ensures the correct insulin dosage, aiding in the efficient processing of sugars.

Consistent Meal Times: Daily meals are beneficial to predict better and manage blood sugar levels. This regularity aids in maintaining a more stable blood glucose profile.

Avoid Sugary Beverages: Drinks with high sugar, such as sodas, can rapidly and significantly increase blood glucose levels. It's best to limit or avoid these.

Monitor for Hypoglycemia: Physical activity can sometimes lead to drops in blood sugar levels. It's crucial to recognize the symptoms of hypoglycemia (low blood sugar) and always to keep quick sugar sources, like glucose tablets, easily accessible.

By adhering to these dietary guidelines, individuals with Type 1 diabetes can better manage their condition and lead healthier lives.

Type 2 Diabetes

Imagine your body's system as a factory. A team creates the essential «keys» known as insulin inside this factory. These keys are crucial for allowing sugar to enter the cells used as fuel. In Type 2 diabetes, although the team continues to produce the keys, the doors to the cells become rusty, affecting their function. As a result, the body either doesn't utilize the insulin effectively or doesn't produce adequate amounts of it. This malfunction leads to an accumulation of sugar in the bloodstream. Type 2 diabetes is more prevalent and can be influenced by diet, physical activity, and genetics. Fortunately, it can be managed efficiently with the right dietary choices, consistent exercise, and sometimes medications.

Dietary Guidelines for Type 2 Diabetes

Focus on Whole Foods: It is advantageous to have a diet high in lean proteins, whole grains, and a range of vegetables. These foods undergo slower digestion and absorption processes in the body, resulting in more stable blood sugar levels.

Limit Refined Sugars: It's wise to exercise

caution with foods with high refined sugar content, like candies, cakes, and other sweet treats. Such foods can cause rapid spikes in blood glucose levels and are best consumed in moderation.

Healthy Fats are Key: Incorporate foods that are sources of healthy fats. Avocados, nuts, and olive oil are excellent examples. These fats promote overall health and do not adversely affect blood sugar levels.

Monitor Portion Sizes: Being mindful of the quantity of food you consume is essential. By regulating portion sizes, you can maintain caloric intake, which aids in weight management — a vital component in effectively managing Type 2 diabetes.

By following these guidelines, individuals with Type 2 diabetes can better control their condition and enhance their overall well-being.

Gestational Diabetes

Gestational diabetes can be likened to a temporary factory operation disruption. This condition arises during pregnancy when a woman's body cannot generate enough «keys» (insulin) to cater to the increased needs of the developing baby. Although this type of diabetes typically resolves after childbirth, it is crucial to manage it effectively. If left unchecked, gestational diabetes can impact the health of both the mother and the baby. The good news is that it can be well-managed with the right dietary choices and maintaining an active lifestyle.

Dietary Guidelines for Gestational Diabetes

Consistent Carbohydrates: To ensure that blood sugar levels remain stable, it's essential to spread your carbohydrate intake evenly throughout your meals.

Choose Nutrient-Dense Snacks: Instead of indulging in snacks with little nutritional value, opt for nutrient-rich snacks. Fruits, yogurt, or a small portion of nuts are great choices.

Stay Hydrated: Maintaining hydration is essential for managing gestational diabetes. Consuming adequate water aids the kidneys in expelling excess sugar from the body via urine, helping to regulate blood sugar levels.

Regular Monitoring is Key: The fluctuations in hormonal levels during pregnancy can render blood sugar levels somewhat erratic. Monitoring them regularly provides insights, allowing for timely dietary adjustments and better-informed food choices.

By adhering to these guidelines, expectant mothers can navigate gestational diabetes more confidently, ensuring the best health outcomes for themselves and their babies.

Why a Diabetic Diet is Crucial?

Understanding diabetes is essential, but knowing how to manage it is the key to leading a healthy and active life. Diet plays a critical part in managing diabetes. Let's delve into why following a diabetic-friendly diet is so crucial for those diagnosed with this condition.

1. Blood Sugar Control:

At the core of diabetes is the body's inability to regulate blood sugar levels. What we eat directly affects these levels. Consuming the right foods in the right amounts can help stabilize blood sugar, preventing dangerous spikes and dips that can lead to complications or immediate health crises.

2. Weight Management:

For many individuals, particularly those with Type 2 diabetes, weight plays a significant role. Being overweight can increase insulin resistance, which makes diabetes symptoms worse. A well-balanced diet can assist in achieving and maintaining a healthy weight, thus easing the management of diabetes.

3. Prevention of Complications:

Diabetes that is not controlled can cause several complications, such as kidney damage, nerve damage, heart disease, and visual issues. By ensuring that the body receives all the vital nutrients it requires to function properly and by avoiding items that worsen diabetic symptoms, a nutritious diet can help prevent these issues.

4. Enhancing Overall Well-being:

A diabetic diet is not just about avoiding sugar. It's about consuming a balanced amount of proteins, fats, and carbohydrates, ensuring adequate intake of vitamins and minerals, and staying hydrated. This diet promotes overall health, boosts energy levels, and enhances mental clarity.

5. Personal Empowerment:

Knowing that you're making informed choices about your diet can be empowering. It gives individuals with diabetes a sense of control over their condition. It also promotes a proactive approach, where one is not merely reacting to symptoms but actively preventing them.

6. Variety is the Spice of Life:

A common misconception is that a diabetic diet is restrictive. On the contrary, it can introduce you to many ingredients and recipes you might not have explored otherwise. It's all about finding the right balance and making informed food choices.

In Conclusion:

The essence of a diabetic diet is to ensure that individuals with diabetes can lead a life as usual and active as anyone else. With careful planning, knowledge, and a dash of culinary creativity, a diabetic diet can be both nutritious and delicious.

As we dive into the recipes in this cookbook, remember the principles outlined in this chapter. Happy cooking, and here's to a healthier you!

Dietary Requirements for Diabetes

Understanding the role of various nutrients is a cornerstone of managing diabetes. Each has a distinct impact on blood sugar levels and overall health. Let's delve into the specifics of carbohydrates, sugars, protein, fats, calories, fiber, and sodium, laying a foundation for making informed dietary choices.

Carbohydrates:

Role: Carbohydrates break down into glucose in the body, impacting blood sugar levels.

Types:

- Complex Carbohydrates (or Starches): Found in foods like whole grains, beans, and legumes. They are digested more slowly, providing a steady energy source.

    - Simple Carbohydrates: Found in fruits, milk, and sugary foods. They are digested quickly, causing a rapid rise in blood sugar.

    - Recommendation: Prioritize complex carbs and be wary of portion sizes. Consider using methods like carbohydrate counting to manage intake.

    ### Sugars:

    Role: Sugar is a type of simple carbohydrate. Blood sugar levels may surge quickly as a result.

    #### Types:

    - Natural Sugars: Found in fruits (fructose) and milk (lactose).

    - Added Sugars: Additional sugars that are added to processed meals and beverages.

        Recommendation: Limit the intake of added sugars. Consume natural sugars in moderation and as part of a balanced meal.

Protein:

Role: Essential for tissue repair, immune function, and muscle building. Doesn't directly impact blood sugar.

Sources: Meat, poultry, fish, dairy, eggs, legumes, tofu, and nuts.

Recommendation: Opt for lean protein sources. Combine protein with carbohydrates during meals to help stabilize blood sugar.

Fats:

Role: Provides energy and supports cell growth. It helps the body absorb specific vitamins.

Types:

- Unsaturated Fats: Beneficial for heart health. Found in olive oil, nuts, and avocados.
- Saturated Fats: Found in animal products. It can raise cholesterol.
- Trans Fats: Found in some processed foods. Able to decrease good cholesterol and increase bad cholesterol.

Recommendation: Prioritize unsaturated fats and limit saturated and trans fats. Like protein, fats can be paired with carbs to slow digestion and stabilize blood sugar.

Calories:

Role: Represents the energy provided by food. Managing calorie intake is essential for weight maintenance, a crucial aspect for many with diabetes.

Recommendation: Be mindful of portion sizes and daily caloric needs, considering age, sex, physical activity, and specific health goals.

Fiber:

Role: Assists in digestion, can help stabilize blood sugar levels and improve cholesterol.

Sources: Whole grains, fruits, vegetables, legumes, and nuts.

Recommendation: Incorporate fiber-rich foods into the diet for their numerous benefits.

Sodium:

Role: Essential for nerve and muscle function but can influence blood pressure.

Sources: Table salt, processed foods, canned goods.

Recommendation: Monitor sodium intake, especially if one has hypertension or is at risk. Opt for low-sodium alternatives and season with herbs and spices.

Essential Nutritional Information:

To manage diabetes effectively, it's crucial to be informed about the nutritional content of foods.

This allows for better decision-making when planning meals or eating out. Reading Food Labels, understanding the Glycemic Index (GI), and consistently monitoring one's reactions to different foods are vital in this journey.

In Conclusion:

Managing diabetes through diet isn't just about counting carbs or avoiding sugar. It's a holistic approach that requires understanding various nutrients and their effects on the body. It is feasible to enjoy a rich, diverse diet that not only improves general well-being but also keeps blood sugar in balance by being aware and making wise decisions.

In the coming chapters, we will explore delicious recipes tailored for people with diabetes, keeping in mind the principles laid out here. Onward to a nourishing culinary journey!

Practical Tips for Diabetes-Friendly Cooking

Eating for diabetes doesn't mean bidding farewell to flavorsome dishes. With the right approach, you can enjoy meals that are as irresistible to the palate as they benefit health. In this chapter, we'll explore techniques to ensure your cooking remains delicious and diabetes-friendly.

1. Mastering Cooking Techniques:

Steam Instead of Fry: Steaming vegetables, fish, and even chicken helps retain nutrients and eliminates the need for added fats in frying. This technique ensures that you get the natural taste of foods with all their beneficial properties intact.

Grill or Broil: Grilling vegetables, lean meats, and fish can create a smoky flavor without adding fats or heavy sauces. Additionally, broiling in an oven can give a similar effect by caramelizing the natural sugars in foods, offering a delightful taste.

Stir-Frying: If done right, stir-frying can be a quick and healthy way to prepare meals. Use a non-stick pan and minimal oil, preferably a more beneficial choice like olive or avocado oil, and toss in an assortment of vegetables with lean proteins.

Slow Cooking: A slow cooker can meld flavors together without adding fats or sugars. This method is excellent for stews, soups, and lean cuts of meats.

2. Exploring a Variety of Flavors:

Herbs and Spices: Herbs and spices have a large world.. Basil, rosemary, thyme, turmeric, cinnamon, and cumin, to name a few, can add a burst of flavor without any added calories or carbs. Spices can also offer additional health benefits; cinnamon has been linked to improved blood sugar levels.

Lemon and Vinegar: A splash of lemon juice or a drizzle of vinegar can elevate the taste of salads, grilled meats, and vegetables. They provide a tangy punch without any detrimental effects on blood sugar.

Natural Extracts: Vanilla, almond, and mint extracts can flavor desserts and drinks without adding sugars.

Salsas and Relishes: Freshly made salsas, using ingredients like tomatoes, onions, cilantro, and chili, can be a delightful addition to grilled meats or as a dip. Similarly, relishes made from pickled vegetables can add a tangy twist.

Reduced-sodium Broths: These can be the foundation for flavorful soups, stews, and even sautéing, cutting down on oil.

In Conclusion:

Cooking for diabetes explores creativity, balancing nutrients while ensuring flavors remain vibrant. With these methods and flavor enhancers, you'll be well on your way to creating meals that meet your palate and your health requirements.

In the upcoming sections, we'll venture into recipes incorporating these methods, marrying taste with nutrition and making every meal a joyous experience.

Strategies to Prevent and Control Diabetes

As we embark on this culinary journey, we must recognize that managing diabetes isn't solely about the foods we eat. It's a holistic approach that intertwines nutrition, lifestyle choices, regular monitoring, and understanding our body's needs. Here, we'll delve into strategies that support blood sugar control and encourage a healthier and more fulfilling life.

1. Weight Management

The Role of Weight in Diabetes:

Excess weight, particularly around the abdomen, can increase the body's resistance to insulin, leading to Type 2 diabetes. This risk can be considerably decreased by reaching and maintaining a healthy weight.

Strategies for Weight Management:

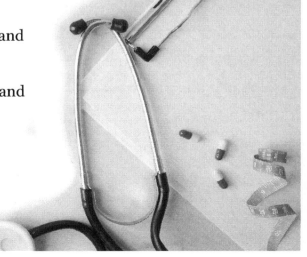

- Balanced Diet: Ensure a mix of carbohydrates, proteins, and healthy fats, focusing on portion sizes.

- Mindful Eating: Recognising your body's hunger signals and fullness can help you stop overeating.

- Limiting Processed Foods: Opt for whole, unprocessed foods that are nutritious and more satisfying.

- Hydration: Drinking water before meals can assist in feeling full and thus reduce overeating.

2. Regular Monitoring and Tests

The Need for Monitoring:

- Consistent monitoring ensures that you are on the right track. It provides real-time feedback, allowing for timely interventions.

- Essential Aspects to Monitor:

- Blood Sugar Levels: Regular self-testing can help determine the effect of foods and activities on your blood sugar.

- HbA1c Test: Taking the average blood sugar over the previous two to three months gives a more comprehensive picture of diabetes management.

- Cholesterol and Blood Pressure: Both can be impacted by diabetes and maintaining them within recommended ranges is vital.

3. Importance of Physical Activity

Exercise and Blood Sugar:

- Physical activity promotes better insulin function and helps manage blood sugar levels.

- Getting Active:

- Aerobic Activities: As jogging, cycling, swimming, or walking...

- Strength Training: Incorporating resistance exercises like weight lifting or using resistance bands.

- Flexibility Exercises: Stretching or yoga can enhance flexibility and muscle tone.

- Consistency is Key: It's not about intensity but regularity. Even 20 minutes a day can make a difference.

Note: Before embarking on any exercise regime, consult your healthcare provider, especially if you have other health concerns.

4. The Role of Sleep

Sleep and Blood Sugar Control:

- Lack of sleep can affect the body's insulin sensitivity, leading to elevated blood sugar levels.

- Strategies for Better Sleep:

- Regular Sleep Schedule: Adhere to a normal bedtime and wake-up schedule daily.

- Sleep Environment: Ensure a calm, dark, and quiet bedroom.

- Limit Caffeine and Alcohol: Particularly at night.

- Unplug: Avoid screens at least an hour before bedtime to help signal the brain that it's time to wind down.

In Conclusion:

While the foods we choose play a pivotal role in managing diabetes, it's the culmination of various lifestyle choices that genuinely pave the way for optimal health. The recipes and meals in this cookbook, complemented by the abovementioned strategies, will set the foundation for a life where diabetes is controlled, not controlled.

In the subsequent chapters, we'll dive deep into delicious recipes that align with these principles. Healthy living never tasted so good!

Shopping Guide: Foods to Embrace and Foods to Avoid

It might be challenging to find your way through the aisles of your neighborhood grocery shop, particularly if you're trying to control your blood sugar. This guide is designed to simplify your shopping experience, helping you make informed decisions that align with your diabetic needs.

1. Foods to Embrace:

Whole Grains:

Why: They are fiber-rich and digest slower than refined grains, gradually increasing blood sugar.

Examples: Quinoa, brown rice, barley, oatmeal, whole grain bread, and pasta.

Lean Proteins:

Why: Proteins are essential for tissue repair and don't directly spike blood sugar.

Examples: Chicken, turkey, fish, tofu, legumes, and eggs.

Healthy Fats:

Why: They provide sustained energy and are essential for vitamin absorption.

Examples: Avocados, nuts, seeds, olive oil, and fatty fish like salmon and trout.

Vegetables:

Why: Packed with vitamins, minerals, and fiber, they are a cornerstone of a balanced diet.

Examples: Leafy greens, bell peppers, broccoli, zucchini, and cauliflower.

Low-Glycemic Fruits:

Why: These fruits impact blood sugar more slowly than their high-glycemic counterparts.

Examples: Berries, apples, pears, oranges, and cherries.

Non-Sweetened Dairy & Alternatives:

Why: They are a good source of calcium and vitamin D.

Examples: Greek yogurt, milk, cheese, almond, and soy milk.

2. Foods to Limit or Avoid:

Sugary Beverages:

Why: They cause rapid spikes in blood sugar.

Examples: Soda, energy drinks, sweetened teas, and fruit juices.

Refined Grains:

Why: They are quickly digested and can rapidly increase blood sugar.

Examples: White bread, white rice, and most pastries.

Processed Snacks:

Why: They often contain refined sugars and unhealthy fats.

Examples: Chips, cookies, and candies.

Trans and Saturated Fats:

Why: They can elevate cholesterol and are not heart-friendly.

Examples: Fried foods, certain margarines, and many processed foods.

High-Sodium Foods:

Why: Excess sodium can raise blood pressure, which is risky for people with diabetes.

Examples: Processed meats, canned soups, and some frozen dinners.

High-Glycemic Fruits:

Why: These fruits can cause a quick rise in blood sugar.

Examples: Pineapple, melons, and ripe bananas.

3. Tips for Smart Shopping:

- Read Labels: Pay attention to terms like «total carbohydrates,» «sugars,» and «fiber.»
- Shop the Perimeter: Fresh produce, dairy, and proteins are often located on the outer edges of the store.
- Plan Ahead: Make a list based on your meal plan for the week.
- Avoid Shopping on an Empty Stomach: This may cause you to make snap decisions that aren't as healthy.
- Choose Fresh Over Processed: Fresh foods generally have fewer additives and hidden sugars.
- Ask for Help: Don't hesitate to ask store employees for guidance or to locate items.

In Conclusion:

With the right approach, Shopping can be a seamless, even enjoyable, experience. This guide is your companion in making choices that are flavorful, nourishing, and supportive of your diabetic needs. As you proceed through this cookbook, you'll find various recipes incorporating these recommended foods, ensuring each meal is a step towards better health.

Before We Begin

Embarking on a culinary journey tailored to specific health needs is an exciting and necessary activity. However, there are a few essential things to remember as you turn the pages of this cookbook and delve into the recipes. We have carefully selected these recipes with diabetes in mind. Therefore, you must speak with your healthcare professional to find out whether certain foods or components are suitable for your particular circumstance.

This book provides meal ideas that may be appropriate for a diabetic diet. It does not constitute medical advice or a treatment plan. Always consult a healthcare professional when managing your diabetes and making nutritional decisions.

Our goal has been to create a collection of delicious and suitable recipes for those monitoring their blood sugar. While we have tried to provide recipes ideal for people with diabetes, individual reactions to certain foods may vary. We encourage readers to consider their body reactions and adjust recipes accordingly. We hope these recipes will become favorites in your kitchen, but we do not take any responsibility for your choices.

All decisions regarding your health, including what you choose to consume, should be made with the consideration and, if necessary, guidance of a healthcare professional. When researching and experimenting, always put your health first and consult professionals if you have any doubts. Let this cookbook inspire and guide you, but remember that the final decisions remain in your hands.

Chapter 2: Breakfast Recipes

Almond Flour Pancakes with Blueberry Sauce

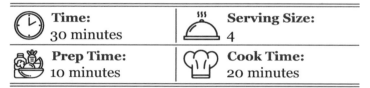 Time: 30 minutes	Serving Size: 4
Prep Time: 10 minutes	Cook Time: 20 minutes

Ingredients:

Pancakes:

- 2 cups almond flour
- Three large eggs
- 1/4 cup unsweetened almond milk
- 1 tsp baking powder
- 1 tsp vanilla extract
- Pinch of salt

Blueberry Sauce:

- 1 cup fresh blueberries
- 1 tbsp chia seeds
- 2 tbsp water
- 1 tsp lemon juice
- 1 tbsp erythritol or another sugar substitute (adjust to taste)

Directions:

1. For the Pancake: Almond flour, eggs, almond milk, baking powder, vanilla extract, and salt should all be combined in a sizable mixing dish. Blend the batter until it's smooth and free of lumps.

2. Preheat a nonstick skillet on medium heat. For each pancake, transfer 1/4 cup of batter to the skillet.

3. Cook for 2-3 minutes on each side or until golden brown.

4. For the Blueberry Sauce: In a small saucepan, combine blueberries, chia seeds, water, lemon juice, and erythritol. Bring to a simmer over medium heat.

5. Continue simmering for 5-7 minutes or until the blueberries break down and the sauce thickens.

6. Serve the pancakes warm, topped with the blueberry sauce.

Nutrition Information:

Calories: 600, **Carbohydrates:** 25g, **Protein:** 20g, **Fat:** 50g, **Sugar:** 10g, **Sodium:** 150mg, **Fiber:** 10g.

Quinoa and Berry Morning Bowl

Time: 35 minutes	Serving Size: 4
Prep Time: 5 minutes	Cook Time: 30 minutes

Ingredients:

- 1 cup quinoa (rinsed   and drained)

- 2 cups water
- 1/2 cup fresh blueberries
- 1/2 cup fresh strawberries, sliced
- 1/4 cup almond slices
- 1 tbsp chia seeds
- 1 tsp vanilla extract
- 2 tbsp erythritol or another sugar substitute (adjust to taste)
- 1 cup unsweetened almond milk (optional for serving)

Directions:

1. Heat the water in a medium saucepan until it starts to boil. After lowering the heat, stir in the quinoa. Once the quinoa is cooked and the water has been absorbed, cover and simmer for 15 minutes.

2. Fluff with a fork after five minutes of cooling off from the heat.

3. Stir in the vanilla extract and erythritol, ensuring even distribution.

4. Divide quinoa among four serving bowls.

5. Top each bowl with blueberries, strawberries, almond slices, and chia seeds.

6. If desired, drizzle unsweetened almond milk over the top before serving.

Nutrition Information:

Calories: 720, **Carbohydrates:** 95g, **Protein:** 25g, **Fat:** 25g, **Sugar:** 15g, **Sodium:** 80mg, **Fiber:** 15g.

Spinach and Feta Breakfast Scramble

⏲ Time: 20 minutes	🍽 Serving Size: 4
🥗 Prep Time: 5 minutes	👨‍🍳 Cook Time: 15 minutes

Ingredients:

- 6 large eggs
- 1/4 cup unsweetened almond milk
- 1 tbsp olive oil
- 1 small onion, finely chopped
- 2 cloves garlic, minced
- 2 cups fresh spinach, chopped
- 1/2 cup crumbled feta cheese
- Salt and pepper to taste
- 1 tsp dried oregano (optional)
- 1/4 cup fresh parsley, chopped; garnish optional.

Directions:

1. Mix the almond milk and eggs in a medium-sized bowl. Suppose using season with oregano, salt, and pepper. Put aside.

2. Warm up the olive oil in a big nonstick skillet set over medium heat. Add the onions and cook for about 3 minutes until they become translucent.

3. Add minced garlic and sauté for another minute.

4. Cook the chopped spinach in the skillet for three to four minutes or until it wilts.

5. Pour the egg mixture over the spinach. Let it sit for a few seconds, and then gently stir with a spatula, pushing the eggs from the edges to the center.

6. When the eggs are about halfway set, sprinkle the crumbled feta.

7. Cook the eggs until they are set, stirring now and then.

8. If preferred, top a hot dish with freshly chopped parsley.

Nutrition Information:

Calories: 720, **Carbohydrates:** 20g, **Protein:** 48g, **Fat:** 50g, **Sugar:** 8g, **Sodium:** 1200mg, **Fiber:** 4g.

Diabetic-friendly Whole Grain Muffins

⏰ Time: 35 minutes	🍽 Serving Size: 12 muffins
🥗 Prep Time: 15	👨‍🍳 Cook Time: 20 minutes

Ingredients:

- 2 cups whole grain flour (like entire wheat or spelled)
- 1 tsp baking soda
- 2 tsp baking powder
- 1/4 tsp salt
- 1/2 cup unsweetened applesauce
- 1/4 cup olive or avocado oil
- 2 large eggs
- A half-cup of almond milk (or other type of milk) without sugar added
- 1 tsp vanilla extract
- one-third cup of pure maple syrup or raw honey
- 1 cup mixed berries (like blueberries, raspberries, or chopped strawberries)

Directions:

1. Set aside a muffin tin (lined with 12 paper liners or lightly greased) and preheat the oven to 375°F (190°C).

2. Combine whole-grain flour, baking soda, baking powder, and salt in a large mixing bowl.

3. Whisk together the eggs, oil, almond milk, vanilla extract, honey, maple syrup, and unsweetened applesauce until smooth.

4. After thoroughly mixing the dry ingredients, add the wet ingredients gradually. Stay submerged.

5. Gently fold in the mixed berries.

6. Fill each muffin cup to about two-thirds full after dividing the batter equally.

7. When a toothpick is placed into the center of a muffin, it should come out clean after 18 to 20 minutes of baking in a preheated oven.

8. After five minutes of cooling in the muffin tray, move the muffins to a wire rack to finish cooling.

Nutrition Information:

Calories: 2288, **Carbohydrates:** 372g, **Protein:** 60g, **Fat:** 72g, **Sugar:** 144g, **Sodium:** 3120mg, **Fiber:** 48g.

Chia Seed Pudding with Fresh Mango

⏰ Time: 4 hours 15 minutes	🍽 Serving Size: 4 servings
🥗 Prep Time: 15 minutes	👨‍🍳 Cook Time: 4 hours

Ingredients:

- 1/4 cup chia seeds
- One cup of unsweetened almond milk (or another kind of milk)
- 1 tsp vanilla extract
- 2 ripe mangos, peeled and diced

Directions:

1. Combine the chia seeds, almond milk, and vanilla extract in a mixing bowl. Stir well.

2. Place a lid or plastic wrap over the bowl in the refrigerator for at least 4 hours, preferably overnight. This lets the liquid seep into the chia seeds, giving them a pudding-like consistency.

3. Once set, stir the pudding well to break up any clumps.

4. Topped with diced mango, serve the chia pudding in individual bowls or glasses.

5. Tip: For an added flavor boost, sprinkle some toasted coconut or chopped nuts on top before serving.

Nutrition Information:

Calories: 552, **Carbohydrates:** 89.5g, **Protein:**

13g, **Fat:** 18.5g, **Sugar:** 45.5g, **Sodium:** 180mg, **Fiber:** 26g.

Broccoli and Cheese Frittata

	Time: 35 minutes		Serving Size: 4 servings
	Prep Time: 10 minutes		Cook Time: 25 minutes

Ingredients:

- 6 large eggs
- 1/4 cup almond milk, unsweetened (or another milk alternative)
- 1 cup broccoli florets, finely chopped
- 1/2 cup of grated cheddar cheese or any other preferred cheese
- 2 tbsp olive oil or unsalted butter
- 1/4 cup diced red bell pepper
- 1/4 cup diced onion
- Salt and black pepper to taste
- Two tablespoons of freshly chopped parsley (optional for garnish)

Directions:

1. Turn the oven on to 375°F, or 190°C.

2. Whisk eggs, almond milk, pepper, and salt in a mixing bowl until smooth.

3. In an oven-safe skillet, preheat the butter or olive oil over medium heat. Add the bell pepper and onions and sauté for 3 minutes or until they are transparent.

4. Add the finely chopped broccoli to the skillet and continue sautéing for another 5 minutes or until the broccoli begins to soften.

5. After combining the egg and milk, evenly distribute it over the vegetables in the skillet.

6. Place the pan in the preheated oven and bake for 15 to 20 minutes or until the top of the frittata begins to brown.

7. Remove from the oven and let it cool for a few minutes before slicing.

8. If preferred, garnish with chopped parsley before serving.

Nutrition Information:

Calories: 840, **Carbohydrates:** 20g, **Protein:** 48g, **Fat:** 60g, **Sugar:** 8g, **Sodium:** 720mg, **Fiber:** 4g.

Overnight Oats with Cinnamon and Apple

	Time: 8 hours 10 minutes		Serving Size: 4 servings
	Prep Time: 10 minutes		Cook Time: 8 hours

Ingredients:

- 2 cups old-fashioned rolled oats
- 2 1/2 cups almond milk (or similar milk substitute) that hasn't been sweetened
- 1 large apple, cored and diced
- 2 tsp ground cinnamon
- 1 tbsp chia seeds
- 1 tsp pure vanilla extract
- 2 tbsp sugar-free maple syrup or sweetener of choice
- A pinch of salt
- Optional toppings: chopped nuts, additional diced apple, or a sprinkle of cinnamon

Directions:

1. Combine rolled oats, chia seeds, ground cinnamon, vanilla extract, sugar-free maple syrup, and a pinch of salt in a large mixing bowl.

2. Gradually pour in the almond milk, mixing well to ensure all ingredients are well combined.

3. Fold in the diced apple pieces.

4. Divide the mixture evenly among four mason

jars or airtight containers.

5. Seal the containers and place them in the refrigerator for at least 8 hours or overnight.

6. Before serving, give each jar a good stir. If you find the consistency too thick, add more almond milk.

7. Garnish with optional toppings if desired.

Nutrition Information:

Calories: 880, **Carbohydrates:** 152g, **Protein:** 28g, **Fat:** 18g, **Sugar:** 32g, **Sodium:** 600mg, **Fiber:** 24g

again after adding a small amount of almond milk if it's too thick.

3. Taste and adjust the sweetness, if necessary, by adding more sugar-free sweetener or stevia.

4. After transferring the smoothie into glasses, serve it right away.

Nutrition Information:

Calories: 480, **Carbohydrates:** 24g, **Protein:** 44g, **Fat:** 22g, **Sugar:** 12g, **Sodium:** 260mg, **Fiber:** 10g.

High-Protein Breakfast Smoothie

🕐 **Time:** 10 minutes	🍽 **Serving Size:** 2 servings
🥗 **Prep Time:** 10 minutes	👨‍🍳 **Cook Time:** 0 minutes

Ingredients:

• One cup of unsweetened almond milk (or another kind of milk)

• 1 scoop (around 30g) of low-carb protein powder (vanilla or unflavored)

• 1 tablespoon chia seeds

• 1 tablespoon natural almond or peanut butter

• 1/2 cup Greek yogurt

(unsweetened and low-fat)

• 1/2 cup mixed berries (like blueberries, raspberries, and strawberries)

• A pinch of ground cinnamon (optional)

• A few ice cubes (optional for a colder smoothie)

• 1 teaspoon sugar-free sweetener or stevia (optional, to taste)

Directions:

1. Place all the ingredients in a high-powered blender.

2. Process the mixture on high until it becomes creamy and smooth. Blend the smoothie

Avocado and Tomato Breakfast Bruschetta

🕐 **Time:** 15 minutes	🍽 **Serving Size:** 4 servings
🥗 **Prep Time:** 10 minutes	👨‍🍳 **Cook Time:** 5 minutes

Ingredients:

• 4 slices of whole-grain bread

• 2 ripe avocados, peeled, pitted, and mashed

• 2 large tomatoes, diced

• 2 tablespoons fresh basil, chopped

• 1 tablespoon olive oil

• 1 garlic clove, minced

• 1 tablespoon lemon juice

• Salt and pepper, to taste

• Optional: Red pepper flakes or freshly grated Parmesan for topping

Directions:

1. Toast the slices of whole-grain bread to your preferred level of crispiness.

2. Whisk together mashed avocados, diced tomatoes, fresh basil, lemon juice, minced garlic, salt, and pepper in a mixing dish. Mix until all the ingredients are well incorporated.

3. Evenly spread the avocado and tomato mixture onto each slice of toasted bread.

4. Drizzle a little olive oil over each bruschetta.

5. Add freshly grated Parmesan cheese or red pepper flakes, if desired.

6. While the toast is still warm, serve it right away.

Nutrition Information:

Calories: 900, **Carbohydrates:** 84g, **Protein:** 20g, **Fat:** 60g, **Sugar:** 12g, **Sodium:** 400mg, **Fiber:** 28g.

Multi-seed Granola with Unsweetened Yogurt

⏱ Time: 40 minutes	🍛 Serving Size: 8 servings
🥗 Prep Time: 10 minutes	👨‍🍳 Cook Time: 30 minutes

Ingredients:

- 2 cups old-fashioned rolled oats
- 1/4 cup flaxseeds
- 1/4 cup chia seeds
- 1/4 cup sunflower seeds
- 1/4 cup pumpkin seeds
- 1/4 cup unsweetened coconut flakes
- 1/4 cup almonds, roughly chopped
- 1/4 cup walnuts, roughly chopped
- 3 tablespoons extra virgin olive oil
- 2 tablespoons unsweetened almond butter
- 1/4 cup sugar-free maple syrup
- 1 teaspoon vanilla extract
- A pinch of salt
- 2 cups unsweetened yogurt for serving

Directions:

1. Turn the oven on to 325°F, or 165°C. Put parchment paper on the bottom of a large baking sheet.

2. Combine rolled oats, flaxseeds, chia, sunflower, pumpkin, coconut flakes, almonds, and walnuts in a large mixing bowl.

3. Warm the olive oil, almond butter, sugar-free maple syrup, and vanilla extract over low heat in a small saucepan. Stir until smooth and well combined.

4. Swirl everything to ensure it is coated after adding the wet liquid to the dry ingredients.

5. Spread the granola mixture in a uniform layer in a thin layer onto the prepared baking sheet.

6. Bake, stirring regularly, for 25 to 30 minutes or until the granola is golden brown.

7. Take it out of the oven and allow it to cool fully. As it cools, the granola will get crunchier.

8. Accompany the granola with plain yogurt. Any extra granola should be kept in an airtight container.

Nutrition Information:

Calories: 2720, **Carbohydrates:** 240g, **Protein:** 80g, **Fat:** 180g, **Sugar:** 32g, **Sodium:** 400mg, **Fiber:** 60g.

Vegetable-Stuffed Omelette

⏱ Time: 20 minutes	🍛 Serving Size: 2 servings
🥗 Prep Time: 10 minutes	👨‍🍳 Cook Time: 10 minutes

Ingredients:

- 4 large eggs
- 1/4 cup skim milk
- Salt and pepper, to taste
- 1 tablespoon olive oil
- 1/4 cup bell pepper, finely diced (a mix of colors)

- 1/4 cup zucchini, finely diced
- 1/4 cup mushrooms, sliced
- 2 tablespoons red onion, finely chopped
- 1/4 cup fresh spinach, chopped
- 1/4 cup cherry tomatoes, halved
- 1/4 cup reduced-fat feta cheese, crumbled (optional)
- Fresh parsley, chopped, for garnish

Directions:

1. Whisk the eggs, skim milk, salt, and pepper in a mixing bowl until well combined.

2. In a nonstick skillet, warm the olive oil over medium heat. Add the red onion, red pepper, zucchini and mushrooms. Sauté for 4-5 minutes or until the vegetables are tender.

3. Ensure the veggies are evenly distributed before pouring the egg mixture. Arrange the cherry tomatoes and spinach on one half of the omelet.

4. Cook the omelet for 4-5 minutes without stirring or until the bottom is lightly golden.

5. Sprinkle the optional feta cheese on the side with the spinach and tomatoes.

6. Carefully fold the omelet in half, covering the spinach and tomatoes.

7. Cook for another 2 minutes, then carefully flip and cook for another 2 minutes on the other side.

8. Transfer to a plate, garnish with fresh parsley, and serve hot.

Nutrition Information:

Calories: 420, **Carbohydrates:** 14g, **Protein:** 26g, **Fat:** 28g, **Sugar:** 9g, **Sodium:** 540mg, **Fiber:** 3g.

Nutty Breakfast Bars

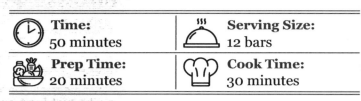

Time: 50 minutes	Serving Size: 12 bars
Prep Time: 20 minutes	Cook Time: 30 minutes

Ingredients:

- 1 cup old-fashioned rolled oats
- 1/2 cup raw almonds, roughly chopped
- 1/2 cup raw walnuts, roughly chopped
- 1/4 cup flaxseeds
- 1/4 cup chia seeds
- 1/4 cup sunflower seeds
- 1/4 cup unsweetened coconut flakes
- 1/4 cup sugar-free maple syrup
- 3 tablespoons extra virgin olive oil
- 1 teaspoon cinnamon
- 1/2 teaspoon nutmeg
- 2 medium eggs, beaten
- A pinch of sea salt

Directions:

1. Set the oven's temperature to 175°C/350°F. Press parchment paper into an 8 × 8-inch baking sheet, leaving a slight overhang for simple removal.

2. Combine rolled oats, almonds, walnuts, flaxseeds, chia, sunflower, and coconut flakes in a large mixing bowl.

3. Mix the sugar-free maple syrup, olive oil, cinnamon, nutmeg, and beaten eggs in a separate bowl until smooth.

4. Mix all ingredients until thoroughly blended after adding the wet mixture to the dry components.

5. Press down hard to achieve a uniform layer after transferring the mixture to the prepared baking pan.

6. Bake for 25 to 30 minutes until the center is set and the sides are golden brown.

7. After letting the bars cool completely in the

pan, take them out and cut them into twelve equal bars.

Nutrition Information:

Calories: 2880, **Carbohydrates:** 192g, **Protein:** 96g, **Fat:** 216g, **Sugar:** 48g, **Sodium:** 240mg, **Fiber:** 60g.

Flaxseed and Raspberry Muffins

	Time: 45 minutes		Serving Size: 12 muffins
	Prep Time: 15 minutes		Cook Time: 30 minutes

Ingredients:

- 2 cups almond flour
- 1/2 cup ground flaxseeds
- 1 teaspoon baking powder
- 1/4 teaspoon sea salt
- 1/4 cup coconut oil, melted
- 1/4 cup sugar-free maple syrup
- 3 large eggs
- 1 teaspoon vanilla extract
- 1 cup fresh raspberries

Directions:

1. Set the oven's temperature to 175°C/350°F. Use paper liners or coconut oil to butter or line a muffin pan.

2. Whisk together almond flour, sea salt, baking powder, and powdered flaxseeds in a large basin.

3. Combine the melted coconut oil, sugar-free maple syrup, eggs, and vanilla extract in another bowl. Until smooth, stir.

4. Until just incorporated, gradually fold the wet ingredients into the dry ingredients.

5. Gently fold in the raspberries.

6. Distribute the batter equally among the muffin cups, filling them to about two-thirds full.

7. A toothpick put into the center of the muffins should come out clean after baking them for 25 to 30 minutes in a preheated oven.

8. Once the muffins are taken out of the oven, let them cool in the pan for five minutes, and then move them to a wire rack to cool completely. They to a wire rack to finish cooling.

Nutrition Information:

Calories: 2160, **Carbohydrates:** 108g, **Protein:** 72g, **Fat:** 180g, **Sugar:** 24g, **Sodium:** 840mg, **Fiber:** 48g.

Calories: 180, **Carbohydrates:** 9g, **Protein:** 6g, **Fat:** 15g, **Sugar:** 2g, **Sodium:** 70mg, **Fiber:** 4g.

Sausage and Pepper Breakfast Casserole (low-fat)

	Time: 1 hours 15 minutes		Serving Size: 8 servings
	Prep Time: 15 minutes		Cook Time: 1 hour

Ingredients:

- 1 pound low-fat turkey sausage
- 1 medium red bell pepper, diced
- 1 medium green bell pepper, diced
- 1 medium yellow onion, diced
- 8 large eggs
- 1/4 cup unsweetened
- almond milk
- 1 teaspoon dried oregano
- 1/2 teaspoon garlic powder
- Salt and pepper to taste
- 1 cup low-fat shredded cheddar cheese

- Fresh parsley, chopped (for garnish)

Directions:

1. Turn the oven on to 375°F, or 190°C. Grease a 9 x 13-inch baking dish very lightly.

2. The turkey sausage should be fried in a big skillet over medium heat, broken up with a spatula as it cooks. Take out of the skillet and pour off any extra grease.

3. In the same skillet, add the diced peppers and onion. Sauté until softened, about 5 minutes.

4. Whisk together eggs, almond milk, oregano, garlic powder, salt, and pepper in a large bowl.

5. Add the cooked sausage and sautéed vegetables to the egg mixture. Stir well to combine.

6. Spoon the mixture into the warm baking dish, then sprinkle the cheese on top.

7. Bake in the oven for 45-50 minutes until the center is set and the edges are slightly golden.

8. Take it out of the oven and give it ten minutes to cool. Before serving, garnish with chopped parsley.

Nutrition Information:

Calories: 1440, **Carbohydrates:** 40g, **Protein:** 136g, **Fat:** 80g, **Sugar:** 20g, **Sodium:** 2320mg, **Fiber:** 8g.

Toasted Almond and Coconut Muesli

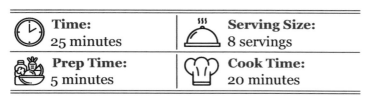 Time: 25 minutes	Serving Size: 8 servings
Prep Time: 5 minutes	Cook Time: 20 minutes

Ingredients:

- 2 cups old-fashioned rolled oats
- 1 cup raw almonds, coarsely chopped
- 1 cup unsweetened shredded coconut
- 2 tablespoons chia seeds
- 2 tablespoons flaxseeds
- 1/2 teaspoon ground cinnamon
- 1/4 teaspoon salt
- 1/4 cup coconut oil, melted
- 2 tablespoons pure maple syrup or another sugar-free sweetener
- 1/2 cup dried berries (blueberries, cranberries, or cherries), unsweetened

Directions:

1. Turn the oven on to 325°F, or 165°C. Line a baking sheet with parchment paper.

2. Combine the rolled oats, chopped almonds, shredded coconut, chia seeds, flaxseeds, cinnamon, and salt in a large mixing bowl.

3. Over the oat mixture, drizzle the melted coconut oil and maple syrup.

4. Evenly spread the mixture over the ready baking sheet.

5. Bake, stirring halfway through, for 18 to 20 minutes in a preheated oven or until the mixture is aromatic and golden brown. Watch closely to prevent over-browning.

6. Remove from the oven and let the muesli cool completely. The mixture will become crunchier as it cools.

7. Once cooled, mix in the dried berries.

8. Keep for no more than two weeks in an airtight container.

Nutrition Information:

Calories: 3280, **Carbohydrates:** 280g, **Protein:** 80g, **Fat:** 220g, **Sugar:** 60g, **Sodium:** 960mg, **Fiber:** 64g.

Chapter 3: Chicken and Turkey Dishes

Grilled Chicken Salad with Balsamic Reduction

 Time: 45 minutes
 Serving Size: 4 servings
 Prep Time: 20 minutes
Cook Time: 25 minutes

Ingredients:

- 4 boneless, skinless chicken breasts
- 2 tablespoons olive oil
- Salt and pepper, to taste
- 1/2 cup (or 8 tablespoons) balsamic vinegar
- 8 cups mixed salad greens (e.g., spinach, arugula, romaine)
- 1 cup cherry tomatoes, halved
- 1/2 cup cucumber, sliced
- 1/4 cup red onion, thinly sliced
- 1/4 cup feta cheese, crumbled (optional)
- 1/4 cup walnuts, toasted
- Fresh basil leaves for garnish

Directions:

1. Preheat the grill to medium-high heat.

2. After massaging the chicken breasts with olive oil, season them with salt and pepper.

3. When the chicken is cooked through and the internal temperature reaches 165°F (74°C), grill it for 6 to 8 minutes on each side. Before slicing, take it off the grill and rest for a few minutes.

4. Balsamic vinegar should be heated to a boil in a saucepan over medium heat. Simmer the vinegar until it reduces by half and takes on the consistency of syrup, reducing heat to low. This will take about 10-12 minutes. Allow to cool.

5. Combine the salad greens, cherry tomatoes, cucumber, and red onion in a large bowl.

6. Divide the salad mixture among 4 plates. Top with the grilled chicken slices.

7. Drizzle each salad with the balsamic reduction. If desired, sprinkle with feta cheese and toasted walnuts.

8. Serve right away after adding some fresh basil leaves as a garnish.

Nutrition Information:

Calories: 1,400, **Carbohydrates:** 67,5g, **Protein:** 120g, **Fat:** 70g, **Sugar:** 30g, **Sodium:** 800mg, **Fiber:** 8g.

Lemon Herb Roasted Turkey Thighs

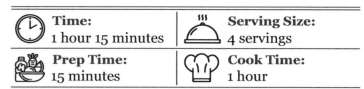 Time: 1 hour 15 minutes	Serving Size: 4 servings
Prep Time: 15 minutes	Cook Time: 1 hour

Ingredients:

- 4 turkey thighs, bone-in, skin-on
- 2 lemons, zested and juiced
- 4 garlic cloves, minced
- 2 tablespoons olive oil
- 2 teaspoons fresh rosemary, finely chopped
- 2 teaspoons fresh thyme, finely chopped
- Salt and black pepper, to taste
- 1/2 cup low-sodium chicken broth

Directions:

1. Turn the oven on to 375°F, or 190°C.

2. Combine lemon zest, lemon juice, minced garlic, olive oil, chopped rosemary, and thyme in a bowl. Mix well to combine.

3. Season the turkey thighs with salt and black pepper. Rub the lemon-herb mixture over the turkey thighs to coat them well.

4. Skin-side up put the turkey thighs in a roasting pan. Fill the pan bottom with the low-sodium chicken broth.

5. The turkey legs are done when they are 165°F (74°C) inside and golden brown. Roast for approximately one hour in the oven with the roasting pan inside.

6. Before serving, take the turkey thighs out of the oven and rest for five to ten minutes.

Nutrition Information:

Calories: 1,800, **Carbohydrates:** 28g, **Protein:** 240g, **Fat:** 80g, **Sugar:** 8g, **Sodium:** 600mg, **Fiber:** 4g.

Chicken Spinach and Feta Stuffed Peppers

Time: 1 hour	Serving Size: 4 servings
Prep Time: 20 minutes	Cook Time: 40 minutes

Ingredients:

- Four large bell peppers (any color), cut off the tops, and throw away the seeds
- One pound of coarsely chopped, skinless, boneless chicken breast
- 1 cup fresh spinach, chopped
- 1/2 cup feta cheese, crumbled
- 1 small onion, finely chopped
- 2 garlic cloves, minced
- 1 tablespoon olive oil
- 1 teaspoon dried oregano
- Salt and black pepper, to taste
- 1 cup low-sodium chicken broth

Directions:

1. Turn the oven on to 375°F, or 190°C.

2. Olive oil should be heated in a big skillet over moderate heat. Sauté the onions and garlic until the onions are transparent.

3. Add the finely chopped chicken to the skillet and cook until no longer pink.

4. Cook the chopped spinach by stirring it in until it wilts. Add some salt, black pepper, and oregano for flavor.

5. Remove from heat and fold in the crumbled feta cheese.

6. Stuff each bell pepper with the chicken-spinach-feta mixture, pressing down gently to pack the filling.

7. Spoon the low-sodium chicken stock around the stuffed peppers in a baking dish.

8. Bake the casserole in the oven for 30 to 35 minutes, or until the peppers are soft,

covered with aluminum foil.

9. Take off the foil and bake for five minutes, just long enough for the tops to lightly brown.

10. Remove from the oven and let them cool for a few minutes before serving.

Nutrition Information:

Calories: 1,440, **Carbohydrates:** 56g, **Protein:** 136g, **Fat:** 72g, **Sugar:** 32g, **Sodium:** 1,400mg, **Fiber:** 16g.

Rosemary Turkey Meatballs

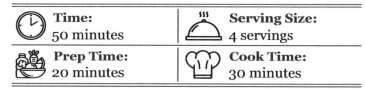 Time: 45 minutes	Serving Size: 4 servings
Prep Time: 15 minutes	Cook Time: 30 minutes

Ingredients:

- 1 lb ground turkey (93% lean)
- 2 tablespoons fresh rosemary, finely chopped
- 1/4 cup almond flour
- 1 egg, lightly beaten
- 2 garlic cloves, minced
- 1 small onion, finely chopped
- Salt and black pepper, to taste
- 1 tablespoon olive oil
- 1/4 cup low-sodium chicken broth

Directions:

1. Combine the ground turkey, chopped rosemary, almond flour, beaten egg, minced garlic, and finely chopped onion in a mixing bowl—season with salt and black pepper. Mix well.

2. Shape the mixture into 16 meatballs, ensuring each is compact and smooth.

3. Place olive oil in a big skillet and heat it over medium heat. When all sides of the meatballs are browned, add them and simmer, turning them over often.

4. After adding the low-sodium chicken broth to the skillet:

5. Cover it.

6. Lower the heat to a simmer.

7. The meatballs should be cooked for 15 to 20 minutes, or until done.

8. Remove from heat and let sit for a few minutes before serving.

Nutrition Information:

Calories: 880, **Carbohydrates:** 20g, **Protein:** 112g, **Fat:** 40g, **Sugar:** 8g, **Sodium:** 600mg, **Fiber:** 4g.

Baked Chicken with Sun-dried Tomato Pesto

Time: 50 minutes	Serving Size: 4 servings
Prep Time: 20 minutes	Cook Time: 30 minutes

Ingredients:

- 4 boneless, skinless chicken breasts
- Salt and black pepper, to taste
- 1/2 cup sun-dried tomatoes (not in oil)
- 1/4 cup fresh basil leaves
- 2 garlic cloves
- 1/4 cup grated Parmesan cheese
- 2 tablespoons olive oil
- 1/4 cup pine nuts or walnuts
- 1/4 cup low-fat feta cheese, crumbled

Directions:

1. Preheat oven to 375°F (190°C).

2. On both sides, sprinkle chicken breasts with salt and black pepper. Kindly put them on an ovenproof dish and keep them aside.

3. In a food processor, pulse together sun-dried

tomatoes, almonds, olive oil, garlic, basil, and grated Parmesan cheese. Pulse until the pesto is smooth.

4. Spread a generous layer of the sun-dried tomato pesto on each chicken breast.

5. Sprinkle crumbled feta cheese over the chicken.

6. Bake for 25 to 30 minutes until the chicken is thoroughly cooked and no longer has any pink in the middle.

7. Let rest for a few minutes before serving.

Nutrition Information:

Calories: 1440, **Carbohydrates:** 40g, **Protein:** 160g, **Fat:** 72g, **Sugar:** 16g, **Sodium:** 1400mg, **Fiber:** 8g.

coat them with the marinade. Let the turkey marinate for at least 10 minutes, preferably up to 30 minutes.

3. Preheat the grill to medium-high heat.

4. Thread the marinated turkey cubes onto the soaked wooden skewers.

5. After putting the turkey skewers on the grill, cook them for 12 to 15 minutes, rotating them halfway through or until the turkey is cooked through and has developed a light sear outside.

6. Once done, remove from the grill and let them rest for a few minutes before serving.

Nutrition Information:

Calories: 920, **Carbohydrates:** 16g, **Protein:** 128g, **Fat:** 36g, **Sugar:** 2g, **Sodium:** 600mg, **Fiber:** 4g.

Garlic Herb Turkey Skewers

	Time: 45 minutes		Serving Size: 4 servings
	Prep Time: 15 minutes		Cook Time: 30 minutes

Ingredients:

- 1 pound of 1-inch-cube-sized turkey breast

- 4 garlic cloves, minced

- 2 tablespoons fresh rosemary, finely chopped

- 2 tablespoons fresh thyme, finely chopped

- 2 tablespoons fresh parsley, finely chopped

- 3 tablespoons olive oil

- Salt and black pepper, to taste

- Water-soaked wooden skewers, soaking for half an hour

Directions:

1. Combine minced garlic, rosemary, thyme, parsley, olive oil, salt, and pepper in a mixing bowl. Mix well to form a marinade.

2. Add the turkey cubes to the bowl and toss to

Spinach and Cheese Stuffed Chicken Breast

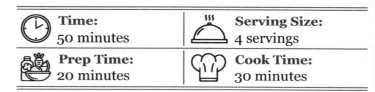

	Time: 50 minutes		Serving Size: 4 servings
	Prep Time: 20 minutes		Cook Time: 30 minutes

Ingredients:

- 4 boneless, skinless chicken breasts

- 1 cup fresh spinach, finely chopped

- 1/2 cup feta cheese, crumbled

- 1/4 cup low-fat ricotta cheese

- 2 garlic cloves,

minced

- 1 tablespoon olive oil

- Salt and pepper, to taste

- 1/2 teaspoon dried oregano

- 1/4 teaspoon red pepper flakes (optional)

Directions:

1. Turn the oven on to 375°F, or 190°C.

2. Combine spinach, feta cheese, ricotta cheese, and minced garlic in a mixing bowl. Mix until all ingredients are well combined.

3. Make a small incision in the middle of every chicken breast, taking care not to slice all the way through.

4. Stuff each chicken breast pocket with the spinach and cheese mixture, distributing it evenly.

5. Sprinkle red pepper flakes, oregano, salt, and pepper on the outside of the chicken breasts.

6. In a large ovenproof skillet, preheat the olive oil over medium heat. When hot, add the chicken breasts and sear for two to three minutes on each side, or until golden brown.

7. Place the skillet in the oven that has been preheated, and bake for 20 to 25 minutes, or until the chicken is cooked through.

8. Remove from the oven and let the chicken sit for five minutes before serving.

Nutrition Information:

Calories: 1040, **Carbohydrates:** 12g, **Protein:** 136g, **Fat:** 48g, **Sugar:** 4g, **Sodium:** 880mg, **Fiber:** 2g.

Zesty Orange Glazed Turkey Medallions

⏱ **Time:** 40 minutes	🍲 **Serving Size:** 4 servings
🥗 **Prep Time:** 10 minutes	👨‍🍳 **Cook Time:** 30 minutes

Ingredients:

• 4 turkey breast medallions (about 6 oz each)

• 1/2 cup freshly squeezed orange juice

• 1/4 cup chicken broth

or water

• 1 tablespoon orange zest

• 2 tablespoons low-sodium soy sauce

• 1 tablespoon olive oil

• 2 garlic cloves, minced

• 1/2 teaspoon fresh

ginger, grated

• 1/4 teaspoon black pepper

• 1 tablespoon chia seeds (to thicken the sauce, optional)

• 2 green onions, chopped (for garnish)

• Fresh parsley (for garnish)

Directions:

1. Whisk together orange zest, orange juice, chicken broth or water, soy sauce, chopped garlic, grated ginger, and black pepper in a mixing bowl. Put aside.

2. Warm the olive oil over medium heat in a large skillet. Add the turkey medallions and cook for 4-5 minutes per side or until browned.

3. Pour the orange mixture over the turkey medallions, and let them simmer.

4. Turn down the heat to low, cover the skillet, and let the medallions cook for 15 to 20 minutes, basting them with the sauce occasionally.

5. If you desire a thicker sauce, add chia seeds and let simmer for 5 more minutes.

6. Once cooked, transfer the turkey medallions to serving plates and drizzle with the orange glaze. Garnish with fresh parsley and sliced green onions.

Nutrition Information:

Calories: 900, **Carbohydrates:** 40g, **Protein:** 120g, **Fat:** 24g, **Sugar:** 20g, **Sodium:** 960mg, **Fiber:** 6g.

Mediterranean Chicken Wrap

Time: 30 minutes	Serving Size: 4 wraps
Prep Time: 15 minutes	Cook Time: 15 minutes

Ingredients:

- 2 boneless, skinless chicken breasts, thinly sliced
- 4 whole grain tortilla wraps
- 1 cup hummus
- 1 cup cherry tomatoes, halved
- 1/2 cucumber, sliced thinly
- 1/2 cup crumbled feta cheese
- One-fourth cup of sliced and pitted Kalamata olives
- 1 tablespoon olive oil
- 2 teaspoons dried oregano
- Salt and pepper to taste
- 1/2 cup fresh parsley, chopped
- Juice of 1 lemon

Directions:

1. Pour the olive oil into a skillet and heat it over medium heat. Add the oregano, salt, pepper, and cut chicken. Cook for 6–7 minutes on each side until the chicken is no longer pink in the center.

2. Drizzle the cooked chicken with fresh lemon juice and set aside to cool slightly.

3. Lay out a tortilla wrap on a flat surface. Spread a quarter of the hummus on the center of the tortilla.

4. Place a portion of the cooked chicken on top of the hummus.

5. Add cherry tomatoes, cucumber slices, feta cheese, and olives.

6. Sprinkle with fresh parsley and roll the tortilla tightly. Repeat with the remaining wraps.

7. Cut each wrap in half diagonally and serve.

Nutrition Information:

Calories: 1520, **Carbohydrates:** 132g, **Protein:** 112g, **Fat:** 60g, **Sugar:** 16g, **Sodium:** 2140mg, **Fiber:** 32g.

Turkey and Vegetable Stir Fry

Time: 35 minutes	Serving Size: 4 servings
Prep Time: 15 minutes	Cook Time: 20 minutes

Ingredients:

- 1 pound turkey breast, thinly sliced
- 2 tablespoons olive oil
- 1 bell pepper (any color), sliced
- 1 zucchini, sliced into half-moons
- 1 carrot, julienned
- 1/2 cup snap peas, trimmed
- 1/2 cup broccoli florets
- 3 cloves garlic, minced
- 1 tablespoon fresh ginger, grated
- 3 tablespoons low-sodium soy sauce
- 1 tablespoon sesame oil
- 1 teaspoon chili flakes (optional)
- 2 green onions, sliced (for garnish)
- 1 tablespoon toasted sesame seeds (for garnish)

Directions:

1. In a large wok or skillet, preheat the olive oil over medium-high heat.

2. Add the thinly sliced turkey breast and stir-fry until lightly browned and cooked. Remove from skillet and set aside.

3. Add garlic ginger, and sauté for about 1 minute or until aromatic in the same skillet.

4. Introduce bell pepper, zucchini, carrot, snap peas, and broccoli to the skillet. Stir-fry for about 7-8 minutes or until vegetables are

tender but still have a crunch.

5. Return the cooked turkey to the skillet. If using, pour in the soy sauce, sesame oil, and chili flakes. Stir well to combine and coat the turkey and vegetables evenly.

6. Cook for another 2-3 minutes, ensuring everything is heated through.

7. Serve the stir fry garnished with sliced green onions and toasted sesame seeds.

Nutrition Information:

Calories: 1420, **Carbohydrates:** 48g, **Protein:** 152g, **Fat:** 72g, **Sugar:** 18g, **Sodium:** 1400mg, **Fiber:** 12g.

Chapter 4: Beef, Pork, and Lamb Delicacies

Beef and Broccoli Stir Fry with Sesame Seeds

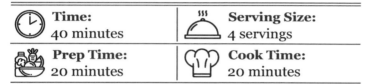

	Time: 40 minutes		Serving Size: 4 servings
	Prep Time: 20 minutes		Cook Time: 20 minutes

Ingredients:

- 1 pound lean beef steak (like sirloin or flank), thinly sliced
- 2 cups broccoli florets
- 1/4 cup beef or vegetable broth
- 3 tablespoons low-sodium soy sauce
- 1 tablespoon sesame oil
- 1 tablespoon oyster sauce
- 2 teaspoons cornstarch

- 2 garlic cloves, minced
- 1-inch ginger, minced
- 2 tablespoons toasted sesame seeds
- 2 tablespoons vegetable oil or canola oil
- 1 red bell pepper, sliced
- 1 tablespoon water (for steaming broccoli)
- 1 green onion, thinly sliced (for garnish)

Directions:

1. In a small bowl, combine the soy sauce, oyster sauce, cornflour, sesame oil, and beef broth. Put away.

2. One tablespoon of vegetable oil should be heated in a big skillet on medium-high heat. Stir-fry the beef pieces until they are browned but not cooked through. Take out and place aside the steak from the grill.

3. Another tablespoon of oil should be added to the same skillet add the garlic and ginger and sauté until fragrant, about 1 minute.

4. Add water and broccoli florets. For about four to five minutes, or until the broccoli is cooked, cover the skillet and let it steam.

5. Remove the cover, add red bell pepper slices, and stir-fry for an additional 2-3 minutes.

6. After the steak is back in the skillet, cover it with the prepared sauce. Stir well, ensuring everything is coated with the sauce. Cook for another 3-4 minutes.

7. Before serving, turn off the heat and toss in the chopped green onions and toasted sesame seeds.

Nutrition Information:

Calories: 1450, **Carbohydrates:** 52g, **Protein:** 144g, **Fat:** 78g, **Sugar:** 16g, **Sodium:** 2400mg, **Fiber:** 10g.

Herb-Crusted Lamb Chops

Time: 45 minutes	Serving Size: 4 servings
Prep Time: 20 minutes	Cook Time: 25 minutes

Ingredients:

- 8 lamb chops, about 3/4-inch thick
- 2 tablespoons olive oil
- 2 garlic cloves, minced
- 2 teaspoons fresh rosemary, finely chopped
- 2 teaspoons fresh thyme, finely chopped
- 2 teaspoons fresh parsley, finely chopped
- 1 teaspoon Dijon mustard
- Salt and pepper, to taste
- Zest of 1 lemon
- 1 tablespoon lemon juice

Directions:

1. Set oven temperature to 400°F or 200°C.

2. Minced garlic, parsley, thyme, rosemary, Dijon mustard, lemon zest, lemon juice, salt, and pepper should all be combined in a mixing bowl. Blend thoroughly until a paste-like texture is achieved.

3. Pat the lamb chops dry using paper towels. Rub each side of the lamb chops with a thin layer of olive oil.

4. Apply the herb mixture to each side of the lamb chops, pressing gently to ensure it adheres.

5. A big ovenproof skillet should be heated to medium-high heat. Once hot, add the lamb chops. Sear each side for about 2-3 minutes until a golden crust forms.

6. After placing the skillet containing the lamb chops in the oven, warm it and roast the chops for 15 to 20 minutes, or until the required doneness is achieved.

7. After cooking, take the lamb chops out of the oven and allow them to rest for about five minutes before serving.

Nutrition Information:

Calories: 1520, **Carbohydrates:** 8g, **Protein:** 136g, **Fat:** 105g, **Sugar:** 2g, **Sodium:** 600mg, **Fiber:** 2g.

Pork Loin with Apple Cider Reduction

Time: 1 hour 15 minutes	Serving Size: 4 servings
Prep Time: 15 minutes	Cook Time: 1 hour

Ingredients:

- 1 pork loin (about 1.5 pounds)
- 1 cup unsweetened apple cider
- 1 cup chicken or vegetable broth
- 2 cloves garlic, minced
- 1 tablespoon olive oil
- Salt and pepper, to taste
- 1 teaspoon dried rosemary
- 1 teaspoon dried thyme
- 2 tablespoons Dijon mustard
- 1 medium-sized onion, thinly sliced

Directions:

1. Turn the oven on to 375°F, or 190°C.

2. In a large skillet, bring the olive oil to a temperature of medium heat. Sauté the garlic and onions until the onions are translucent.

3. Season the pork loin with thyme, rosemary, salt, and pepper. Add to the skillet and sear for 3–4 minutes on each side or until golden brown.

4. Move the pork loin to a baking tray and drizzle with Dijon mustard.

5. Pour apple cider and broth into the skillet to deglaze, ensuring to scrape up any browned bits. Allow the mixture to simmer and reduce by half.

6. Pour the reduced liquid over the pork loin in the baking dish.

7. After 45 to 50 minutes of roasting, the pork loin should be 145°F (63°C) inside. Take it out of the oven and give it ten minutes to rest before slicing. Drizzle the reduced sauce over the pork when serving.

Nutrition Information:

Calories: 1420, **Carbohydrates:** 40g, **Protein:** 140g, **Fat:** 60g, **Sugar:** 24g, **Sodium:** 560mg, **Fiber:** 3g.

Spiced Beef Kebabs

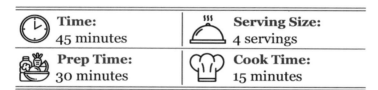

	Time: 45 minutes		Serving Size: 4 servings
	Prep Time: 30 minutes		Cook Time: 15 minutes

Ingredients:

- 1 pound of lean beef cubes, sliced into 1-inch pieces
- 2 tablespoons olive oil
- 1 teaspoon ground cumin
- 1 teaspoon paprika
- 1/2 teaspoon ground turmeric
- 1/4 teaspoon cayenne pepper
- 2 cloves garlic, minced
- 1 tablespoon fresh

lemon juice
- Salt and pepper, to taste
- One medium red bell pepper, sliced into 1-inch segments
- 1 medium-sized zucchini, cut into 1-inch rounds
- Eight skewers, either wooden or metal (if wooden, soak in water for half an hour beforehand)minutes prior)

Directions:

1. In a mixing bowl, combine olive oil, cumin, paprika, turmeric, cayenne pepper, garlic, lemon juice, salt, and pepper. Mix well to form a marinade.

2. Add the beef cubes to the marinade, ensuring they are well-coated. Allow them to marinate for at least 20 minutes or overnight in the refrigerator.

3. Turn the heat up to medium-high on the grill or grill pan.

4. Thread beef cubes onto the skewers, alternating with pieces of red bell pepper and zucchini rounds.

5. After the skewers are on the grill, roast them on each side for 6–7 minutes or until the meat is cooked to your preference.

6. Remove from the grill and let them rest for a few minutes before serving.

Nutrition Information:

Calories: 1220, **Carbohydrates:** 16g, **Protein:** 128g, **Fat:** 68g, **Sugar:** 8g, **Sodium:** 240mg, **Fiber:** 4g.

Mint and Garlic Marinated Lamb Steaks

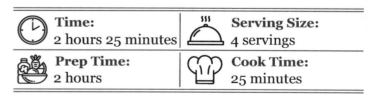

	Time: 2 hours 25 minutes		Serving Size: 4 servings
	Prep Time: 2 hours		Cook Time: 25 minutes

Ingredients:

- 4 lamb steaks (about 6 ounces each)
- 1/4 cup fresh mint leaves, finely chopped
- 4 cloves garlic, minced
- 3 tablespoons olive oil
- 1 tablespoon lemon juice
- Salt and pepper, to taste

- 1 teaspoon dried oregano
- Zest of 1 lemon

Directions:

1. Combine mint, garlic, olive oil, lemon juice, salt, pepper, oregano, and lemon zest in a bowl. Mix well to form the marinade.

2. Place lamb steaks in a large resealable plastic bag or a shallow dish. Pour the marinade over the lamb, ensuring each steak is well-coated.

3. Let the lamb marinate for at least two hours by covering the dish or sealing the bag and placing it in the refrigerator.

4. Set the grill pan or grill to medium-high heat.

5. Remove the lamb from the marinade, letting the excess drip off. Place the steaks on the grill.

6. Grill lamb steaks for 10-12 minutes on each side or until they reach your desired level of doneness.

7. Remove from the grill and let them rest for a few minutes before serving.

Nutrition Information:

Calories: 1640, **Carbohydrates:** 12g, **Protein:** 140g, **Fat:** 110g, **Sugar:** 2g, **Sodium:** 400mg, **Fiber:** 2g.

Pork Tenderloin with Mushroom Gravy

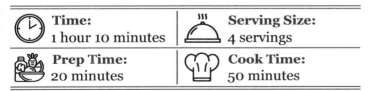

⏱ Time: 1 hour 10 minutes	🍲 Serving Size: 4 servings
🥗 Prep Time: 20 minutes	👨‍🍳 Cook Time: 50 minutes

Ingredients:

- 1 pork tenderloin (about 1 to 1.5 pounds)
- 2 tablespoons olive oil
- Salt and pepper, to taste
- 1 small onion, finely diced
- 2 cloves garlic, minced
- 2 cups sliced button mushrooms
- 1 tablespoon fresh thyme leaves
- 2 tablespoons all-purpose flour or almond flour for a lower-carb option
- 2 cups low-sodium chicken broth

Directions:

1. Turn the oven on to 375°F, or 190°C.

2. Add salt and pepper to the pork tenderloin to season it.

3. One tablespoon of olive oil should be heated in a sizable ovenproof skillet over medium-high heat. The pork should be seared for two to three minutes on each side or until golden brown.

4. Once the pork has reached an internal temperature of 145°F (63°C), roast it for 25 to 30 minutes in the oven. When finished, move to a platter and tent with foil.

5. Transfer the leftover olive oil to the identical skillet. Sauté the onions until they become transparent.

6. Stir the mushrooms and garlic together, allowing them to release their juice and start to become colored.

7. After adding the flour and stirring, sauté the mushrooms for one to two minutes.

8. Stirring constantly while adding the chicken broth helps prevent lumps from forming. The gravy should be allowed to simmer for around five to seven minutes to thicken.

9. Add the thyme leaves after seasoning with salt and pepper to taste.

10. Serve the pork tenderloin sliced with mushroom gravy on top.

Nutrition Information:

Calories: 1320, **Carbohydrates:** 34g, **Protein:** 112g, **Fat:** 78g, **Sugar:** 8g, **Sodium:** 800mg, **Fiber:** 4g.

Slow-Cooked Beef Ragu with Zucchini Noodles

Time: 8 hours 20 minutes	Serving Size: 4 servings
Prep Time: 20 minutes	Cook Time: 8 hours

Ingredients:

- 1.5 pounds beef chuck roast, cut into large chunks
- 1 tablespoon olive oil
- 1 medium onion, finely chopped
- 3 cloves garlic, minced
- 1 can (14 oz) crushed tomatoes
- 1/4 cup red wine (optional)

- 2 teaspoons dried Italian seasoning
- Salt and pepper, to taste
- 4 large zucchinis, spiralized into noodles
- Grated Parmesan cheese (optional for garnish)
- Fresh basil leaves for garnish

Directions:

1. Place the olive oil in a big skillet and heat it to medium-high. Brown the beef chunks on all sides, about 2-3 minutes per side.

2. Transfer the beef to a slow cooker.

3. In the same skillet, add onions and sauté until translucent. Simmer the garlic for a further thirty seconds.

4. Add the crushed tomatoes, red wine (if using), and Italian seasoning to the skillet, stirring to combine and deglaze the pan—season with salt and pepper.

5. Cover the steak in the slow cooker with the tomato mixture.

6. After 8 hours of low cooking under cover, the beef should be soft and easily shredded.

7. Once done, use two forks to shred the beef in the sauce.

8. In a big pan, cook the zucchini noodles over medium heat for three to four minutes or until they are somewhat soft. Avoid overcooking them since they may get overly tender.

9. Serve the beef ragu over the zucchini noodles. If preferred, garnish with freshly chopped basil leaves and grated Parmesan cheese.

Nutrition Information:

Calories: 1600, **Carbohydrates:** 48g, **Protein:** 128g, **Fat:** 96g, **Sugar:** 28g, **Sodium:** 880mg, **Fiber:** 12g.

Lamb and Spinach Curry (low-fat version)

Time: 1 hour 20 minutes	Serving Size: 4 servings
Prep Time: 20 minutes	Cook Time: 1 hour

Ingredients:

- 1 pound lean lamb, diced
- 1 large onion, finely chopped
- 3 cloves garlic, minced
- 1-inch fresh ginger, grated
- 2 tablespoons tomato paste
- One cup of canned diced tomatoes without

additional salt

- 2 cups fresh spinach, chopped
- 1 tablespoon curry powder
- 1 teaspoon ground turmeric
- 1 teaspoon ground cumin
- 1/4 tsp chili powder, or more according to taste

- 1 cup low-fat plain yogurt
- 1 tablespoon olive oil
- Salt to taste
- Fresh coriander leaves, for garnish

Directions:

1. In a large skillet, heat the olive oil over medium-high heat. Brown the lamb chunks all over after adding them. Remove the lamb and set aside.

2. In the same skillet, sauté the onion until translucent. Cook the ginger and garlic for one to two more minutes after adding them.

3. Stir in the tomato paste, diced tomatoes, curry powder, turmeric, cumin, and chili powder. Return the lamb to the skillet and mix well.

4. Once the lamb is cooked, reduce heat, cover, and simmer for about 45 minutes.

5. Add the chopped spinach and heat for approximately five minutes or until it wilts.

6. Take off the heat and thoroughly mix in the yogurt. To taste, adjust the salt.

7. Serve the curry hot, garnished with fresh coriander leaves.

Nutrition Information:

Calories: 1200, **Carbohydrates:** 52g, **Protein:** 104g, **Fat:** 64g, **Sugar:** 28g, **Sodium:** 640mg, **Fiber:** 12g.

Grilled Pork Salad with Lime Dressing

🕐 Time: 45 minutes	🍽 Serving Size: 4 servings
🥗 Prep Time: 25 minutes	👨‍🍳 Cook Time: 20 minutes

Ingredients:

- 1 pound lean pork tenderloin
- 6 cups mixed salad greens (e.g., romaine, arugula, spinach)
- 1 red bell pepper, thinly sliced
- 1 cucumber, sliced
- 1/4 cup fresh cilantro, chopped
- 2 green onions, thinly sliced
- 1 tablespoon olive oil
- Salt and pepper to taste
- Lime Dressing:
- Juice of 2 limes
- 2 tablespoons olive oil
- 1 clove garlic, minced
- 1 teaspoon honey (or a suitable low-carb sweetener)
- Salt and pepper to taste

Directions:

1. Preheat the grill to medium-high heat. Rub the pork tenderloin with olive oil, salt, and pepper.

2. Grill the pork for about 18-20 minutes, turning occasionally, until cooked through but still slightly pink in the center. Let it rest for a few minutes before slicing thinly.

3. While the pork is grilling, prepare the lime dressing: Mix the lime juice, olive oil, honey, garlic, salt, and pepper in a small bowl. Adapt the seasoning to your taste.

4. Mix the green onions, cucumber, cilantro, red bell pepper, and greens in a big bowl.

5. Add the sliced grilled pork to the salad.

6. Over the salad, drizzle with the lime dressing and toss lightly to mix.

7. Serve right away.

Nutrition Information:

Calories: 1400, **Carbohydrates:** 44g, **Protein:** 112g, **Fat:** 88g, **Sugar:** 24g, **Sodium:** 640mg, **Fiber:** 12g.

Beef Teriyaki with Steamed Veggies

Time: 50 minutes	 Serving Size: 4 servings
Prep Time: 20 minutes	Cook Time: 30 minutes

Ingredients:

- 1 pound lean beef sirloin, thinly sliced
- 1/4 cup low-sodium soy sauce
- 2 tablespoons erythritol or another diabetic-friendly sweetener
- 1 tablespoon sesame oil
- 1 tablespoon fresh ginger, grated
- 2 cloves garlic, minced
- 4 cups mixed veggies (broccoli, bell peppers, snow peas, and carrots)
- 1 tablespoon olive oil
- 2 green onions, sliced for garnish
- 1 tablespoon sesame seeds, for garnish

Directions:

1. Combine the low-sodium soy sauce, erythritol, sesame oil, ginger, and garlic in a mixing bowl. Stir until the sweetener dissolves.

2. Add the sliced beef to the marinade, ensuring that every slice is well-coated. Allow it to marinate for 15 minutes.

3. While the beef is marinating, start steaming the mixed veggies. Heat the water in a big pot fitted with a steamer insert until it boils. Place the mixed veggies in the steamer, cover, and steam for about 5-7 minutes or until veggies are tender but still have a crunch. Remove from heat.

4. The olive oil should be heated in a skillet over medium heat. Stir-fry the marinated beef slices for three to four minutes or until the steak reaches the desired doneness (discard any leftover marinade).

5. Serve the beef teriyaki over the steamed veggies. Garnish with green onions and sesame seeds.

Nutrition Information:

Calories: 1200, **Carbohydrates:** 56g, **Protein:** 100g, **Fat:** 60g, **Sugar:** 20g, **Sodium:** 1280mg, **Fiber:** 16g.

Lamb Tagine with Apricots

Time: 2 hours 15 minutes	Serving Size: 4 servings
Prep Time: 15 minutes	Cook Time: 2 hours

Ingredients:

- 1 pound lean lamb, cubed
- 1 cup dried apricots, roughly chopped
- 1 onion, finely chopped
- 2 cloves garlic, minced
- 2 tablespoons olive oil
- 2 cups low-sodium beef or vegetable broth
- 1 teaspoon ground cumin
- 1 teaspoon ground coriander
- 1/2 teaspoon ground cinnamon
- 1/4 teaspoon ground turmeric
- Salt and pepper to taste
- 2 tablespoons fresh cilantro, chopped (for garnish)
- 2 tablespoons almond slivers (optional)

Directions:

1. Warm the olive oil over medium heat in a large saucepan or tagine. Sauté the garlic and onions until they are transparent.

2. Brown the lamb cubes on all sides after adding them.

3. Once browned, add cumin, coriander, cinnamon, turmeric, salt, and pepper. Mix well until the lamb is well-coated with the spices.

4. Add the chopped apricots and mix again.

5. Pour in the low-sodium broth and bring to a simmer. After it begins to simmer, turn down the heat to low, cover, and stew steadily for about two hours, stirring now and then.

6. Remove from heat once the lamb is tender and the apricots have softened. If the tagine is too liquid, you can increase the heat and cook uncovered for a few minutes to reduce it.

7. Serve hot, garnished with fresh cilantro and almond slivers if desired.

Nutrition Information:

Calories: 1760, **Carbohydrates:** 140g, **Protein:** 100g, **Fat:** 90g, **Sugar:** 80g, **Sodium:** 680mg, **Fiber:** 20g.

Balsamic Glazed Pork Ribs

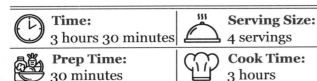

Time: 3 hours 30 minutes	Serving Size: 4 servings
Prep Time: 30 minutes	Cook Time: 3 hours

Ingredients:

- 2 pounds pork ribs
- 1/4 cup balsamic vinegar
- 1/4 cup apple cider vinegar (for tang without as much sugar)
- 3 tablespoons olive oil
- 2 tablespoons low-sodium soy sauce
- 1 tablespoon Dijon mustard
- 2 cloves garlic, minced
- 1 teaspoon dried rosemary
- Salt and pepper to taste
- 2 tablespoons chia seeds (to thicken the glaze, optional)

Directions:

1. Preheat oven to 300°F (150°C).

2. In a mixing bowl, combine balsamic vinegar, apple cider vinegar, olive oil, soy sauce, Dijon mustard, minced garlic, rosemary, salt, and pepper. Stir to create the marinade.

3. Ensure the pork ribs are evenly coated on both sides, place them in a baking dish, and cover with the marinade.

4. Bake the baking dish for 2.5 hours in the preheated oven, covered with aluminium foil.

5. Take the ribs out of the oven after 2.5 hours, and pour the juices into a saucepan. If using chia seeds, add them now. Reduce the heat to low and simmer until the sauce thickens and doubles in size.

6. Raise the oven's temperature to 190°C, or 375°F. Brush the reduced glaze onto the ribs and return them to the oven (uncovered) for 30 minutes, or until they have a caramelized layer.

7. Take out of the oven, give it a 10-minute rest, and then serve.

Nutrition Information:

Calories: 2000 , **Carbohydrates:** 40g , **Protein:** 160g, **Fat:** 140g, **Sugar:** 20g, **Sodium:** 680mg, **Fiber:** 8g.

Sizzling Beef and Pepper Fajitas

Time: 40 minutes	Serving Size: 4 servings
Prep Time: 20 minutes	Cook Time: 20 minutes

Ingredients:

- 1 pound lean beef steak, thinly sliced
- 1 red bell pepper, sliced
- 1 green bell pepper, sliced
- 1 yellow bell pepper, sliced
- 1 onion, thinly sliced
- 2 tablespoons olive oil
- 2 cloves garlic, minced

- 1 teaspoon cumin
- 1 teaspoon paprika
- Salt and black pepper to taste
- 4 whole-grain tortillas (or low-carb alternatives)
- 1/4 cup chopped fresh cilantro (for garnishing purposes only)
- 1 lime, cut into wedges

Directions:

1. Sliced meat, garlic, cumin, paprika, salt, and pepper should all be combined in a big bowl. To ensure the spices are evenly covered on the beef, thoroughly mix.

2. Warm the olive oil in a big skillet or pan over medium-high heat.

3. The beef should be added to the hot oil and cooked for three to four minutes or until browned. Take out and place aside the steak from the skillet.

4. Sliced onions and bell peppers should be added to the same skillet. Sauté for about 5-7 minutes or until softened.

5. Stir thoroughly and add the cooked steak back to the skillet. Cook for an additional 2-3 minutes.

6. Warm the tortillas as per package instructions.

7. To serve, divide the beef and pepper mixture evenly among the tortillas. Serve with lime wedges on the side and garnish with fresh cilantro.

Nutrition Information:

Calories: 1120, **Carbohydrates:** 92g, **Protein:** 108g, **Fat:** 36g, **Sugar:** 16g, **Sodium:** 620mg, **Fiber:** 12g.

Rosemary and Lemon Lamb Stir Fry

🕐 Time: 35 minutes	🍽 Serving Size: 4 servings
🥗 Prep Time: 15 minutes	👨‍🍳 Cook Time: 20 minutes

Ingredients:

- 1 pound lean lamb, thinly sliced
- 2 tablespoons fresh rosemary, finely chopped
- 1 lemon, zested and juiced
- 2 tablespoons olive oil
- 2 cloves garlic, minced
- 1 red bell pepper, thinly sliced
- 1 green bell pepper, thinly sliced
- 1 small red onion, thinly sliced
- 2 cups snap peas, trimmed
- Salt and black pepper to taste
- 1 tablespoon low-sodium soy sauce
- 2 green onions, chopped (for garnish)

Directions:

1. Combine lamb slices, rosemary, lemon zest, and half of the lemon juice in a large mixing bowl. Allow to marinate for ten minutes after tossing to coat.

2. Heat one tablespoon of olive oil in a large wok or skillet over medium-high heat. After adding the lamb, stir-fry it for four to five minutes or until it is almost cooked and browned. After removing the lamb, place it aside.

3. The same wok should have the olive oil that is left added to it. Sauté the garlic for about a minute after it has been mixed in with the oil. Include the red bell pepper, the green bell pepper, the red onion, and the snap peas in the dish. Stir fry the veggies for five to seven minutes or until soft but somewhat crunchy.

4. Return the lamb to the wok. Add the soy sauce and the remaining lemon juice. After giving everything a good stir, cook for two to three minutes.

5. Season with salt and black pepper as needed.

6. Add some finely chopped green onions as a garnish and serve hot.

Nutrition Information:

Calories: 1120, **Carbohydrates:** 44g, **Protein:** 104g, **Fat:** 60g, **Sugar:** 20g, **Sodium:** 540mg, **Fiber:** 12g.

Pork and Pineapple Skewers

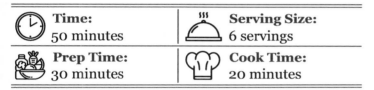

🕐 Time: 50 minutes	🍽 Serving Size: 6 servings
🥗 Prep Time: 30 minutes	👨‍🍳 Cook Time: 20 minutes

Ingredients:

- 1.5 pounds lean pork tenderloin, cut into 1-inch cubes

- 2 cups fresh pineapple chunks

- 2 red bell peppers, sliced into pieces measuring 1 inch

- 1/4 cup low-sodium soy sauce

- 2 tablespoons olive oil

- 1 tablespoon apple cider vinegar

- 2 cloves garlic, minced

- 1 teaspoon ground black pepper

- 1/2 teaspoon ground cumin

- Metal or wooden skewers; if wooden, soak in water for half an hour before grilling.

Directions:

1. In a mixing bowl, combine soy sauce, olive oil, apple cider vinegar, garlic, black pepper, and cumin to create the marinade.

2. Add the pork cubes to the marinade, ensuring each piece is well coated. Allow to marinate, preferably in the fridge, for at least 20 minutes.

3. Preheat the grill to medium-high heat.

4. Assemble the skewers by alternating between pork cubes, pineapple chunks, and red bell pepper pieces.

5. Place the skewers on the grill and cook for about 10 minutes on each side or until the pork is cooked and has a slight char on the outside.

6. Before serving, remove from the grill and let sit for a few minutes.

Nutrition Information:

Calories: 1440, **Carbohydrates:** 72g, **Protein:** 180g, **Fat:** 48g, **Sugar:** 48g, **Sodium:** 960mg, **Fiber:** 12g.

Chapter 5: Fish and Seafood Selections

Herb-crusted salmon with Asparagus

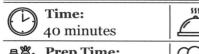 Time: 40 minutes	Serving Size: 4 servings
Prep Time: 15 minutes	Cook Time: 25 minutes

Ingredients:

- 4 salmon fillets (about 6 ounces each)
- 1 bunch fresh asparagus, trimmed
- 3 tablespoons olive oil, divided
- 2 garlic cloves, minced
- 1/4 cup fresh parsley, finely chopped
- 1/4 cup fresh dill, finely chopped
- 1 tablespoon lemon zest
- 2 tablespoons lemon juice
- 1/4 teaspoon black pepper
- 1/4 teaspoon sea salt

Directions:

1. Set oven temperature to 400°F, or 205°C.

2. Garlic, parsley, dill, and lemon zest are to be combined with two tablespoons of olive oil, salt, and black pepper in a bowl that may be used for mixing. Create the herb crust by thoroughly combining the ingredients.

3. Placing the salmon fillets on a baking sheet lined with parchment paper is the first step.

4. Generously brush each salmon fillet with the herb crust mixture.

5. Mix the remaining olive oil (1 tablespoon) and lemon juice (1 tablespoon) with the Asparagus in a separate bowl. Arrange the Asparagus around the salmon on the baking sheet.

6. Take the baking sheet out of the oven when the Asparagus is soft and the salmon flakes easily with a fork.

7. Remove from the oven and serve immediately.

Nutrition Information:

Calories: 1520, **Carbohydrates:** 20g, **Protein:** 192g, **Fat:** 80g, **Sugar:** 8g, **Sodium:** 1000mg, **Fiber:** 12g.

Lemon Butter Grilled Shrimp

Time: 25 minutes	Serving Size: 4 servings
Prep Time: 15 minutes	Cook Time: 10 minutes

Ingredients:

- 1 lb large shrimp,   peeled and deveined

- 3 tablespoons unsalted butter, melted
- 1 large lemon, zested and juiced
- 3 garlic cloves, minced
- 1/4 teaspoon black

pepper
- 1/4 teaspoon sea salt
- 1 tablespoon fresh parsley, finely chopped
- 1 tablespoon olive oil

Directions:

1. Preheat your grill to medium-high heat.

2. Melted butter, lemon zest, lemon juice, minced garlic, salt, and black pepper should all be combined in a bowl. Mix well to create the lemon butter sauce.

3. To keep the prawns from sticking to the grill, lightly coat them with olive oil.

4. Place shrimp on the grill and cook for 2-3 minutes on each side until they turn pink.

5. Once the shrimp are almost done grilling, brush them with lemon butter sauce. Allow them to grill for an additional minute to soak up the flavors.

6. Remove shrimp from the grill and transfer them to a serving plate.

7. Serve immediately, scattering any leftover lemon butter sauce on top and finishing with fresh parsley.

Nutrition Information:

Calories: 1120, **Carbohydrates:** 8g, **Protein:** 92g, **Fat:** 80g, **Sugar:** 2g, **Sodium:** 1780mg, **Fiber:** 1g.

Tuna and Olive Pasta Salad

Time: 35 minutes	Serving Size: 6 servings
Prep Time: 20 minutes	Cook Time: 15 minutes

Ingredients:

- 8 oz whole wheat penne pasta
- Two cans (5 oz each) of drained tuna in water
- 1 cup cherry tomatoes, halved
- Half a cup of pitted and sliced black olives
- 1/4 cup red onion, finely chopped
- 2 tablespoons extra virgin olive oil
- 2 tablespoons red wine vinegar
- 1 garlic clove, minced
- 1 teaspoon dried oregano
- Salt and pepper to taste
- 1/4 cup fresh parsley, chopped
- 2 tablespoons grated Parmesan cheese (optional)

Directions:

1. To ensure pasta is al dente, follow the cooking instructions on the packaging. After draining, rinse with cold water to allow it to cool.

2. Put the cooked pasta, tuna, cherry tomatoes, black olives, and red onion in a big mixing basin.

3. The dressing is made by whisking together the olive oil, red wine vinegar, oregano, minced garlic, salt, and pepper in a separate bowl.

4. After adding the dressing to the spaghetti mixture, gently toss to blend.

5. To let the flavors merge, refrigerate for a minimum of one hour.

6. Before serving, sprinkle with fresh parsley and, optionally, grated Parmesan cheese.

Nutrition Information:

Calories: 1620, **Carbohydrates:** 176g, **Protein:**

120g, **Fat:** 44g, **Sugar:** 16g, **Sodium:** 1650mg, **Fiber:** 28g.

Seared Scallops with Garlic Spinach

Time: 25 minutes	**Serving Size:** 4 servings
Prep Time: 10 minutes	**Cook Time:** 15 minutes

Ingredients:

- 12 large sea scallops, side muscle removed
- 2 tablespoons olive oil
- Salt and freshly ground black pepper should be added to taste.
- 4 garlic cloves, minced
- 8 cups baby spinach
- 1/4 cup of chicken broth or dry white wine
- 1 lemon, zested and juiced
- 2 tablespoons fresh parsley, finely chopped

Directions:

1. Over a heat level somewhere between medium and high, warm one tablespoon of olive oil in a big skillet. Put one tablespoon of olive oil in a large skillet and heat it over medium-high heat until it's shimmering. Once hot, add scallops and sear until a golden crust forms on both sides, about 2 minutes per side. Take the scallops out of the pan and put them to the side.

2. Put the last tablespoon of olive oil in the skillet you used earlier.

3. Add minced garlic and sauté for about 1 minute, until fragrant.

4. Gradually add the spinach to the skillet, allowing each batch to wilt before adding more—season with salt and pepper.

5. Using white wine or chicken broth, deglaze the skillet, scraping away any brown pieces

from the bottom. Let it simmer for 2 minutes.

6. Return the scallops to the skillet, then add lemon zest, lemon juice, and parsley. Stir gently to combine and coat the scallops in the sauce.

7. Serve immediately with scallops on a bed of garlic spinach.

Nutrition Information:

Calories: 520, **Carbohydrates:** 24g, **Protein:** 40g, **Fat:** 28g, **Sugar:** 4g, **Sodium:** 680mg, **Fiber:** 6g.

Cajun Spiced Catfish with Mango Salsa

Time: 30 minutes	**Serving Size:** 4 servings
Prep Time: 15 minutes	**Cook Time:** 15 minutes

Ingredients:

- 4 catfish fillets (about 6 oz each)
- 2 tablespoons olive oil
- 2 teaspoons Cajun seasoning
- Salt to taste
- For the Mango Salsa:
- 1 ripe mango, peeled, pitted, and diced
- 1 medium red bell
- pepper, finely diced
- 1/4 cup red onion, finely chopped
- 1 jalapeño, seeds removed and finely chopped
- 2 tablespoons fresh cilantro, chopped
- Juice of 1 lime
- Salt and pepper to taste

Directions:

1. Mix all the mango salsa ingredients in a mixing basin. Toss until well combined, then refrigerate while you prepare the catfish.

2. Turn on the medium heat and preheat a grill or grill pan.

3. Rub each catfish fillet with olive oil and season with Cajun seasoning and salt.

4. After putting the catfish fillets on the grill, cook them on each side for 5 to 7 minutes or until they are opaque and flake readily with a fork.

5. Remove the catfish from the grill and rest for a few minutes.

6. Serve catfish hot with a generous topping of mango salsa.

Nutrition Information:

Calories: 500, **Carbohydrates:** 26g, **Protein:** 32g, **Fat:** 28g, **Sugar:** 16g, **Sodium:** 240mg, **Fiber:** 4g.

Grilled Mackerel with Lemon Herb Dressing

Time: 25 minutes	Serving Size: 4 servings
Prep Time: 10 minutes	Cook Time: 15 minutes

Ingredients:

- 4 fresh mackerel fillets
- 2 tablespoons olive oil
- Salt and pepper to taste
- For the Lemon Herb Dressing:
- Zest and juice of 1 lemon
- 1/4 cup extra-virgin olive oil
- 2 tablespoons fresh parsley, finely chopped
- 1 tablespoon fresh dill, finely chopped
- 1 clove garlic, minced
- Salt and pepper to taste

Directions:

1. Preheat your grill to medium-high heat.

2. Lightly brush mackerel fillets with olive oil and season both sides with salt and pepper.

3. Grill the mackerel fillets on each side for about 5-7 minutes until they are cooked through and have grill marks.

4. While the mackerel is grilling, prepare the lemon herb dressing. Mix the olive oil, parsley, dill, garlic, lemon zest, and lemon juice in a small bowl. Season with salt and pepper to taste.

5. Once the mackerel is cooked, transfer to serving plates and drizzle the lemon herb dressing.

6. Serve right away with steaming veggies or mixed greens on the side.

Nutrition Information:

Calories: 450, **Carbohydrates:** 2g, **Protein:** 36g, **Fat:** 32g, **Sugar:** 1g, **Sodium:** 90mg, **Fiber:** 0.5g.

Prawn and Zucchini Noodle Stir Fry

Time: 30 minutes	Serving Size: 4 servings
Prep Time: 15 minutes	Cook Time: 15 minutes

Ingredients:

- 400g fresh prawns, peeled and deveined
- 4 medium zucchinis, spiralized into noodles
- 2 tablespoons olive oil
- 3 cloves garlic, minced
- 1 red bell pepper, thinly sliced
- 1 carrot, julienned
- 2 green onions, chopped
- 1 tablespoon fresh ginger, minced
- Two tablespoons of tamari or low-sodium soy sauce (for gluten-free)
- 1 tablespoon sesame oil
- 1 tablespoon sesame seeds (optional)
- Fresh cilantro for garnish (optional)
- Red pepper flakes (optional, for a bit of heat)
- Salt and pepper to taste

Directions:

1. The olive oil should be heated in a large skillet or wok over medium-high heat.

2. When aromatic, add the ginger and garlic to the skillet and sauté.

3. Cook the prawns in the skillet for 3–4 minutes or until they turn pink. Remove prawns and set them aside.

4. Transfer the red bell pepper and carrot to the same skillet. Cook until they start to get tender, about 3 minutes.

5. Stir in the zucchini noodles, ensuring everything is combined.

6. Pour in the low-sodium soy sauce or tamari and sesame oil. Stir to combine.

7. Add the cooked prawns to the skillet and toss everything together until well mixed and heated.

8. If desired, finish by sprinkling with sesame seeds, green onions, fresh cilantro, and red pepper flakes—season with salt and pepper to taste.

9. Serve immediately.

Nutrition Information:

Calories: 230, **Carbohydrates:** 10g, **Protein:** 25g, **Fat:** 10g, **Sugar:** 5g, **Sodium:** 320mg, **Fiber:** 3g.

Baked Cod with Pesto and Cherry Tomatoes

⏲ **Time:** 35 minutes	🍽 **Serving Size:** 4 servings
🥗 **Prep Time:** 10 minutes	👨‍🍳 **Cook Time:** 25 minutes

Ingredients:

- 4 cod fillets (about 150g each)
- 2 tablespoons olive oil
- Salt and pepper, to taste
- 4 tablespoons pesto (preferably homemade or a low-sodium store-bought version)
- 200g cherry tomatoes, halved
- 1 clove garlic, minced
- 2 tablespoons fresh basil, chopped (for garnish)
- 1 lemon, cut into wedges (for serving)

Directions:

1. In a bowl, the following ingredients should be mixed:

2. Cherry tomatoes

3. Minced garlic

4. One tablespoon of olive oil

5. A pinch of salt and pepper

6. Toss until well coated.

7. When placing the cod fillets in a baking dish, make sure there is adequate space between each one. On top of the fillets, drizzle the fillets with the remaining tablespoon of olive oil. Add a dash of salt and a little pepper to each fillet before cooking.

8. Spread a tablespoon of pesto on top of each cod fillet.

9. Scatter the cherry tomatoes mixture around the cod in the baking dish.

10. When the cod flakes easily with a fork, roughly 20 to 25 minutes should pass, depending on how hot the oven is.

11. Take it out of the oven and give it a few minutes to cool.

12. Serve the baked cod hot, garnished with fresh basil and a wedge of lemon.

Nutrition Information:

Calories: 260, **Carbohydrates:** 6g, **Protein:** 27g, **Fat:** 13g, **Sugar:** 3g, **Sodium:** 200mg, **Fiber:** 1g.

Spicy Tuna Patties

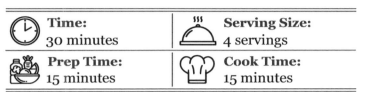

	Time: 30 minutes		Serving Size: 4 servings
	Prep Time: 15 minutes		Cook Time: 15 minutes

Ingredients:

- 2 drained 5-ounce cans of tuna each in water
- 1 large egg, lightly beaten
- 1/4 cup almond flour
- 2 green onions, finely chopped
- 1/4 cup finely chopped bell pepper (red or yellow for color)
- 1 tablespoon fresh lime juice
- 2 teaspoons sriracha or hot sauce (adjust based on your preference)
- 1/4 teaspoon black pepper
- 1 tablespoon of cooking olive or avocado oil
- Lime wedges and fresh cilantro for garnish

Directions:

1. Drained tuna, beaten egg, almond flour, bell pepper, green onions, lime juice, sriracha or hot sauce, and black pepper should all be combined in a big mixing dish. Blend until all components are thoroughly combined.

2. Shape the mixture into 4 equal-sized patties.

3. Heat the olive or avocado oil in a non-stick skillet over medium heat.

4. Carefully place the tuna patties in the skillet. Cook for 6-7 minutes on each side or until golden brown patties are cooked through.

5. Remove the patties from the skillet and place them on a plate lined with paper towels to remove excess oil.

6. Serve the spicy tuna patties hot with lime wedges and a sprinkle of fresh cilantro.

Nutrition Information:

Calories: 180, **Carbohydrates:** 4g, **Protein:** 25g, **Fat:** 8g, **Sugar:** 1g, **Sodium:** 230mg, **Fiber:** 2g.

Lobster Salad with Avocado and Greens

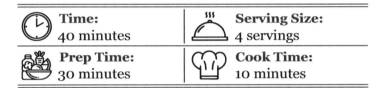

	Time: 40 minutes		Serving Size: 4 servings
	Prep Time: 30 minutes		Cook Time: 10 minutes

Ingredients:

- 2 lobster tails (about 8-10 oz each), steamed and meat removed
- 2 ripe avocados, diced
- 4 cups mixed salad greens (like arugula, spinach, and baby romaine)
- 1/2 cup cherry tomatoes, halved
- 1/4 cup fresh cilantro, chopped
- 1 lemon, zest and juice
- 2 tablespoons extra-virgin olive oil
- 1 tablespoon apple cider vinegar
- Salt and pepper to taste
- 1/4 cup thinly sliced red onion
- 1 tablespoon chia seeds (optional)

Directions:

1. Begin by preparing the dressing: Mix the olive oil, apple cider vinegar, lemon zest, juice, salt, and pepper in a small bowl until thoroughly blended. Put aside.

2. Toss the mixed salad greens, diced avocado, cherry tomatoes, cilantro, and sliced red onion in a large mixing bowl.

3. Chop the steamed lobster meat into bite-sized pieces and add to the salad mixture.

4. After making the dressing, drizzle it over the salad and toss lightly to moisten all the ingredients.

5. Evenly distribute the salad across four dishes.

6. If desired, sprinkle chia seeds on each salad for a crunch and nutritional boost.

7. Serve immediately.

Nutrition Information:

Calories: 300, **Carbohydrates:** 14g, **Protein:** 24g, **Fat:** 18g, **Sugar:** 3g, **Sodium:** 210mg, **Fiber:** 8g.

Chapter 6: Vegetarian and Vegan Varieties

Spinach and Mushroom Quiche (egg-free)

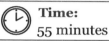 **Time:** 55 minutes	**Serving Size:** 8 servings
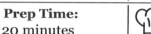 **Prep Time:** 20 minutes	**Cook Time:** 35 minutes

Ingredients:

- 1 prepared pie crust (store-bought or homemade)
- 2 cups fresh spinach, chopped
- 1 cup button mushrooms, sliced
- 1/2 cup onion, finely chopped
- 2 cloves garlic, minced
- 1 block (14 oz.) firm tofu, drained and pressed
- 1/4 cup unsweetened almond milk (or any plant-based milk)
- 2 tbsp nutritional yeast
- 1 tsp dried oregano
- 1/2 tsp turmeric powder (for color)
- Salt and pepper to taste
- 1 tbsp olive oil

Directions:

1. Turn the oven on to 375°F, or 190°C.

2. With a pan over medium heat, preheat the olive oil. Continue the cooking process after adding the onion and garlic, and wait for the onion to become transparent.

3. When the mushrooms release their moisture and start to turn a light brown, add them and simmer.

4. Add the spinach and cook until wilted. Remove from heat and set aside.

5. Tofu, almond milk, nutritional yeast, oregano, turmeric, black salt (if using), and salt and pepper to taste should all be combined in a food processor. Blend until smooth and creamy.

6. Combine the tofu mixture with the sautéed vegetables. Mix well.

7. After preparing the pie crust, pour the ingredients into it and distribute it evenly.

8. Bake for 35 to 40 minutes in a preheated oven or until the filling is set and the top is golden brown.

9. Let cool for ten minutes, then cut into slices and serve.

Nutrition Information:

Calories: 180, **Carbohydrates:** 16g, **Protein:** 9g, **Fat:** 9g, **Sugar:** 2g, **Sodium:** 220mg, **Fiber:** 3g.

Vegan Lentil and Vegetable Curry

	Time: 55 minutes		Serving Size: 6 servings
	Prep Time: 15 minutes		Cook Time: 40 minutes

Ingredients:

- 1 cup rinsed and drained dried lentils, either brown or green

- 1 can (14 oz.) diced tomatoes, undrained

- 1 large carrot, diced

- 1 bell pepper, chopped (any color)

- 1 medium-sized zucchini, diced

- 1 onion, finely chopped

- 3 cloves garlic, minced

- 2 cups vegetable broth or water

- 1 can (14 oz.) coconut milk

- 2 tbsp curry powder

- 1 tsp ground turmeric

- 1 tsp ground cumin

- Half a teaspoon of red chili flakes (or to taste)

- Salt and pepper to taste

- 2 tbsp olive or coconut oil

- Fresh cilantro for garnish (optional)

Directions:

1. Prepare the oil in a large saucepan by heating it over medium heat. Sauté the garlic and onions until they are evident in the pan.

2. Add the carrot, bell pepper, and zucchini. Sauté for another 5 minutes.

3. Add the chili flakes, curry powder, turmeric, and cumin and stir. Cook for a minute until fragrant.

4. Add the lentils, diced tomatoes, vegetable broth or water, and coconut milk to the pot. Stir to combine.

5. After bringing to a boil, turn down the heat. Cover and let simmer for 30-35 minutes, or until the lentils are tender and the vegetables are cooked.

6. Season with salt and pepper to taste.

7. If preferred, top the heated dish with freshly chopped cilantro. This curry pairs wonderfully with brown rice or cauliflower rice for a complete diabetic-friendly meal.

Nutrition Information:

Calories: 290, **Carbohydrates:** 33g, **Protein:** 11g, **Fat:** 13g, **Sugar:** 7g, **Sodium:** 290mg, **Fiber:** 11g.

Stuffed Bell Peppers with Quinoa and Veggies

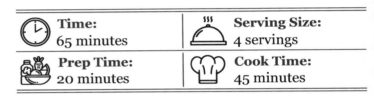

	Time: 65 minutes		Serving Size: 4 servings
	Prep Time: 20 minutes		Cook Time: 45 minutes

Ingredients:

- 4 large bell peppers (any color)

- 1 cup cooked quinoa

- 1 cup black beans, drained and rinsed

- 1 cup diced zucchini

- 1 cup diced tomatoes (canned or fresh)

- 1/2 cup corn kernels (frozen or fresh)

- 1 onion, finely chopped

- 2 cloves garlic, minced

- 2 tbsp olive oil

- 1 tsp ground cumin

- 1 tsp paprika

- Salt and pepper to taste

- 1/4 cup fresh chopped cilantro (optional)

- 1/4 cup shredded vegan cheese (optional)

Directions:

1. Turn the oven on to 375°F, or 190°C.

2. Cut off the bell peppers' tops to extract the seeds and membranes. Put away.

3. The olive oil should be heated in a big skillet over medium heat. Add the onions and garlic, sautéing until translucent.

4. Stir in the zucchini, and cook for 3-4 minutes.

5. Add the black beans, diced tomatoes, corn, cumin, and paprika—coat for an additional five minutes, stirring thoroughly to mix.

6. Add the cooked quinoa and season with pepper and salt after mixing. After cooking for two more minutes, turn off the heat. Mix in the chopped cilantro, if using.

7. Carefully stuff each bell pepper with the quinoa and veggie mixture. The filled peppers should be put in a roasting tray.

8. Sprinkle the tops with vegan cheese if desired.

9. Bake the peppers for 35 to 40 minutes, or until soft, while covering the baking dish with aluminium foil.

10. Please remove it from the oven and let it cool down a little before serving.

Nutrition Information:

Calories: 280, **Carbohydrates:** 45g, **Protein:** 9g, **Fat:** 8g, **Sugar:** 8g, **Sodium:** 200mg, **Fiber:** 10g.

Grilled Tofu Steaks with Chimichurri

⏰	Time: 50 minutes	🍽	Serving Size: 4 servings
🥗	Prep Time: 30 minutes	👨‍🍳	Cook Time: 20 minutes

Ingredients:

- 1 block (14 oz) of firm or extra-firm tofu
- 2 tbsp olive oil
- Salt and pepper to taste
- For the Chimichurri:
- 1 cup fresh parsley, finely chopped
- 1/2 cup fresh cilantro, finely chopped
- 2 cloves garlic, minced
- 1/4 cup olive oil
- 2 tbsp red wine vinegar
- 1/2 tsp red pepper flakes
- Salt and pepper to taste

Directions:

1. To begin, press the tofu by wrapping it in a fresh kitchen towel and setting something heavy on top (such as a can or a skillet). Let it sit for at least fifteen minutes to get rid of extra water.

2. After pressing, slice the tofu block into 1/2-inch thick steaks.

3. Add salt and pepper to each tofu steak after sprinkling it with olive oil. Preheat your grill or grill pan over medium heat. Once hot, grill the tofu steaks on each side for 5-7 minutes until they have distinct grill marks and are golden brown.

4. Make the chimichurri while the tofu is grilling: Olive oil, red wine vinegar, red pepper flakes, parsley, cilantro, and garlic should all be combined in a bowl. Add salt and pepper to taste, then thoroughly mix everything.

5. Once the tofu steaks are done grilling, transfer them to a plate and generously drizzle with the chimichurri sauce. Serve immediately.

Nutrition Information:

Calories: 275, **Carbohydrates:** 4g, **Protein:** 11g, **Fat:** 23g, **Sugar:** 1g, **Sodium:** 15mg, **Fiber:** 1g.

Eggplant and Tomato Casserole

🕐 Time: 1 hour 15 minutes	🍽 Serving Size: 6 servings
🧺 Prep Time: 15 minutes	👨‍🍳 Cook Time: 1 hour

Ingredients:

- 2 medium eggplants, sliced into 1/2-inch rounds
- 3 large tomatoes, cut into 1/2-inch rounds
- 1/4 cup olive oil
- 2 cloves garlic, minced
- 1 tsp dried oregano
- 1 tsp dried basil
- 1/4 tsp red pepper flakes (optional)
- Salt and pepper to taste
- 1/4 cup fresh parsley, chopped
- 2 tbsp fresh basil, chopped for garnish

Directions:

1. Turn the oven on to 375°F, or 190°C.

2. Olive oil, garlic, dried oregano, dried basil, red pepper flakes (if using), salt, and pepper should all be combined in a big bowl.

3. Brush each slice of eggplant and tomato with the olive oil mixture, ensuring both sides are well-coated.

4. Slices of aubergine should be layered in a casserole dish, then slices of tomato. Continue until you have used up every piece.

5. Sprinkle the top with chopped parsley and a bit more salt and pepper.

6. With the foil covering it, bake the casserole dish for fifty minutes.

7. After 50 minutes, when the top starts to have a hint of color, remove the foil and bake for 10 minutes.

8. Remove from the oven and let it cool slightly. Garnish with fresh basil before serving.

Nutrition Information:

Calories: 120, **Carbohydrates:** 15g, **Protein:** 2g, **Fat:** 7g, **Sugar:** 7g, **Sodium:** 10mg, **Fiber:** 6g.

Vegan Thai Green Curry with Veggies

🕐 Time: 40 minutes	🍽 Serving Size: 4 servings
🧺 Prep Time: 10 minutes	👨‍🍳 Cook Time: 30 minutes

Ingredients:

- 2 tbsp coconut oil
- 3 tbsp green curry paste (ensure vegan-friendly)
- 1 can (14 oz.) full-fat coconut milk
- 1 cup vegetable broth
- 2 carrots, thinly sliced
- 1 red bell pepper, sliced
- 1 cup snap peas, halved
- 1 small zucchini, sliced into half-moons
- 1 small eggplant, diced
- 1 tablespoon soy sauce or tamari (make sure it's gluten-free if needed)
- 1 tbsp brown sugar or coconut sugar
- 1/2 cup fresh Thai basil, roughly torn
- 2 green onions, chopped for garnish
- 1 red chili, sliced for garnish (optional)

Directions:

1. In a large pot or wok, heat coconut oil over medium heat. Add the green curry paste and sauté for about 2 minutes, until fragrant.

2. After pouring in the coconut milk and the vegetable broth, stir the mixture well so that the curry paste is evenly distributed.

3. Add the aubergine and carrots once the mixture starts to simmer. Cook for approximately five minutes.

4. Add the bell pepper, snap peas, and zucchini to the pot. Stir well.

5. Mix in tamari or soy sauce and sugar, adjusting to taste.

6. Let the curry simmer for 15-20 minutes or until the vegetables are tender.

7. Just before serving, stir in the Thai basil,

letting it wilt slightly in the hot curry.

8. Serve hot, garnished with green onions and optional red chili slices.

Nutrition Information:

Calories: 280, **Carbohydrates:** 22g, **Protein:** 4g, **Fat:** 21g, **Sugar:** 8g, **Sodium:** 400mg, **Fiber:** 6g.

Spaghetti Squash with Tomato Basil Sauce

⏰ **Time:** 60 minutes	🍽 **Serving Size:** 4 servings
🥗 **Prep Time:** 10 minutes	👨‍🍳 **Cook Time:** 50 minutes

Ingredients:

• 1 medium-sized spaghetti squash (around 3-4 lbs)

• 2 tbsp olive oil, divided

• Salt and pepper, to taste

• 4 cloves garlic, minced

• 1 small red onion, finely chopped

• 28 ounces (one can) of smashed tomatoes without salt

• 1/2 cup fresh basil leaves, chopped

• 1 tsp dried oregano

• 1/2 tsp red pepper flakes (optional)

• For added cheesiness, add 2 tablespoons of nutritional yeast.

• Fresh basil leaves for garnish

Directions:

1. Set oven temperature to 400°F or 200°C.

2. Scoop out the seeds after cutting the spaghetti squash in half lengthwise. Add salt and pepper to taste and drizzle with one tablespoon of olive oil. Place the squash cut side down on a baking sheet.

3. Bake the spaghetti squash for around forty minutes or until it becomes soft and easily shredded with a fork.

4. Prepare the tomato basil sauce while the squash is roasting in the oven. Warm up the remaining tablespoon of olive oil in a big skillet set over medium heat.

5. Add the minced garlic and chopped onion, sautéing until translucent, about 5 minutes.

6. If using, pour in the crushed tomatoes, chopped basil, oregano, and red pepper flakes. After bringing the sauce to a simmer, cook it for fifteen minutes. Add more salt and pepper to taste.

7. If using, stir in the nutritional yeast and cook for another 2-3 minutes.

8. Once the spaghetti squash is ready, use a fork to shred the inside to create «spaghetti strands gently.»Transfer to serving plates.

9. Pour the tomato basil sauce over the spaghetti squash strands and garnish with fresh basil leaves.

10. Serve immediately.

Nutrition Information:

Calories: 180, **Carbohydrates:** 30g, **Protein:** 5g, **Fat:** 7g, **Sugar:** 10g, **Sodium:** 60mg, **Fiber:** 7g.

Spiced Tempeh Tacos with Avocado Lime Crema

⏰ **Time:** 45 minutes	🍽 **Serving Size:** 4 servings
🥗 **Prep Time:** 15 minutes	👨‍🍳 **Cook Time:** 30 minutes

Ingredients:

• 8 oz tempeh, crumbled

• 1 tbsp olive oil

• 2 cloves garlic,

minced

- 1 small red onion, chopped
- 1 red bell pepper, diced
- 2 tsp ground cumin
- 1 tsp smoked paprika
- 1/2 tsp chili powder
- Salt and pepper, to

taste

- 8 small corn tortillas
- 2 avocados
- Juice of 1 lime
- 2 tbsp chopped fresh cilantro
- 1 small jalapeño, seeds removed and finely diced (optional)

Directions:

1. The olive oil should be heated in a big skillet over medium heat. Add the minced garlic, chopped onion, and diced bell pepper. Sauté until the onions are translucent.

2. Add the crumbled tempeh to the skillet. Season with cumin, I smoked paprika, chili powder, salt, and pepper. Cook for 10 to 12 minutes, stirring periodically, or until the tempeh turns golden and begins to crisp up.

3. While the tempeh cooks, prepare the avocado lime crema. Combine the avocados, lime juice, cilantro, and jalapeño in a blender. Blend until smooth—season with salt to taste.

4. Warm the corn tortillas according to package instructions.

5. To assemble, spread a dollop of avocado lime crema on each tortilla. Top with the spiced tempeh mixture.

6. Serve immediately, garnishing with additional chopped cilantro if desired.

Nutrition Information:

Calories: 420, **Carbohydrates:** 46g, **Protein:** 16g, **Fat:** 23g, **Sugar:** 5g, **Sodium:** 80mg, **Fiber:** 11g.

Spinach and Chickpea Coconut Curry

🕐 **Time:** 40 minutes	🍽 **Serving Size:** 4 servings
🥗 **Prep Time:** 10 minutes	👨‍🍳 **Cook Time:** 30 minutes

Ingredients:

- 2 tbsp coconut oil
- 1 medium onion, finely chopped
- 3 cloves garlic, minced
- 1-inch ginger, grated
- 2 tsp ground turmeric
- 1 tsp ground cumin
- 1 tsp ground coriander
- 1/4 tsp cayenne (or more, according to

taste)

- One can of 14 ounces of rinsed and drained chickpeas
- 1 can (14 oz) full-fat coconut milk
- 200g fresh spinach, roughly chopped
- 1 tbsp lime juice
- Salt to taste
- Fresh cilantro for garnish

Directions:

1. Melt the coconut oil over medium heat in a deep pan or large saucepan. Add the onion and simmer for about 5 minutes when it turns transparent.

2. Add the minced garlic and grated ginger to the pot and sauté for an additional minute or two or until aromatic.

3. Add the cayenne pepper, cumin, coriander, and ground turmeric and stir. To give the spices time to bloom, cook for two minutes.

4. Chickpeas and coconut milk should be added to the pot. Stir well to ensure the chickpeas are coated with the spiced coconut mixture.

5. After bringing the mixture to a simmer, cook it for 20 minutes.

6. Once the spinach has wilted and cooked through, stir in the chopped spinach and simmer.

7. After turning off the heat, whisk in the lime juice. To taste, adjust the salt.

8. Serve the curry piping hot, garnished with fresh cilantro, and enjoy.

Nutrition Information:

Calories: 380, **Carbohydrates:** 32g, **Protein:** 9g, **Fat:** 27g, **Sugar:** 6g, **Sodium:** 80mg, **Fiber:** 8g.

Roasted Vegetable and Farro Salad

Time: 50 minutes	Serving Size: 4 servings
Prep Time: 20 minutes	Cook Time: 30 minutes

Ingredients:

- 1 cup farro, rinsed and drained
- 2 cups water
- 1 medium zucchini, diced
- 1 red bell pepper, diced
- 1 yellow bell pepper, diced
- 1 red onion, chopped
- 2 tbsp olive oil
- Salt and pepper to taste
- 2 tbsp balsamic vinegar
- 1 tbsp Dijon mustard
- 1 clove garlic, minced
- 1/4 cup fresh basil, chopped
- 1/4 cup fresh parsley, chopped
- Juice of 1 lemon
- 2 tbsp pine nuts (optional)

Directions:

1. Set oven temperature to 400°F, or 205°C.

2. Stir the farro and water together in a saucepan. After bringing the farro to a boil, reduce the heat and continue to simmer it for 25 to 30 minutes or until it has reached the desired consistency.

3. On a large baking sheet, combine the red peppers, red onion, and zucchini. Olive oil should be drizzled over the mixture before it is mixed—season with salt and pepper. Spread vegetables in an even layer and roast in the oven for 20-25 minutes or until tender and slightly caramelized.

4. Balsamic vinegar, Dijon mustard, minced garlic, lemon juice, salt, and pepper should all be combined in a small basin. This will be your dress.

5. Cooked farro, roasted veggies, chopped parsley, and basil should all be combined in a big bowl. After adding a drizzle of dressing, toss to mix.

6. Serve the salad garnished with pine nuts if desired.

Nutrition Information:

Calories: 310, **Carbohydrates:** 52g, **Protein:** 8g, **Fat:** 9g, **Sugar:** 6g, **Sodium:** 60mg, **Fiber:** 9g.

Chapter 7: Beans, Grains, and Legumes

Black Bean and Corn Salad

Time: 25 minutes	**Serving Size:** 6 servings
Prep Time: 20 minutes	**Cook Time:** 5 minutes

Ingredients:

- 2 cans (15 ounces each) of rinsed and drained black beans
- One cup of fresh, frozen, or canned corn kernels
- 1 red bell pepper, diced
- 1/2 red onion, finely chopped
- 1/2 cup fresh cilantro, chopped
- 2 limes, juiced
- 2 tbsp olive oil
- 1 tsp ground cumin
- Salt and pepper to taste
- 1 avocado, diced (optional)
- 1 jalapeño, seeded and finely chopped (optional for added heat)

Directions:

1. If using frozen corn, cook according to package instructions, then let cool.

2. In a big bowl, combine black beans, corn, red onion, red pepper, and cilantro.

3. Mix the lime juice, olive oil, cumin, salt, and pepper in a different, smaller bowl. You will dress like this.

4. After adding the dressing to the black bean mixture, toss to mix.

5. If using, gently fold in the diced avocado and jalapeño.

6. Refrigerate for at least an hour before serving to allow flavors to meld.

Nutrition Information:

Calories: 220, **Carbohydrates:** 35g, **Protein:** 9g, **Fat:** 6g, **Sugar:** 3g, **Sodium:** 300mg, **Fiber:** 11g.

Lentil and Spinach Stuffed Tomatoes

Time: 55 minutes	**Serving Size:** 4 servings
Prep Time: 20 minutes	**Cook Time:** 35 minutes

Ingredients:

- 4 large tomatoes
- 1 cup cooked green lentils
- 2 cups fresh spinach, chopped
- 1/2 onion, finely chopped
- 2 garlic cloves, minced
- 1/4 cup feta cheese
- (optional for a vegan alternative)
- 2 tbsp olive oil
- 1/2 tsp dried basil or oregano
- Salt and pepper to taste
- Fresh parsley or basil for garnish

Directions:

1. Turn the oven on to 375°F, or 190°C.

2. Slice off the tops of the tomatoes, then carefully remove the insides while preserving the shell. Remove the scooped tomato flesh and set aside.

3. Put some olive oil in a pan and bring it to medium heat. After adding the onion and garlic, cook until the onion becomes translucent.

4. Cook the chopped spinach until it wilts after adding it.

5. Add the lentils, scooped-out tomato flesh, dried basil or oregano, salt, and pepper. Cook for another 5 minutes, stirring occasionally.

6. Take off the heat and, if using, whisk in the feta cheese.

7. Carefully stuff each tomato with the lentil-spinach mixture, pressing down gently to pack the filling.

8. The filled tomatoes should be put on a baking tray and covered with foil.

9. Bake for 25 to 30 minutes, or until the tomatoes are soft, in an oven that has been warmed.

10. Before serving, garnish with basil or parsley that is fresh.

Nutrition Information:

Calories: 220, **Carbohydrates:** 28g, **Protein:** 10g, **Fat:** 8g, **Sugar:** 6g, **Sodium:** 90mg, **Fiber:** 10g.

Quinoa and Roasted Veggie Bowl

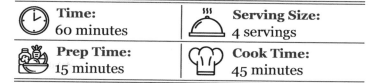

Time: 60 minutes	Serving Size: 4 servings
Prep Time: 15 minutes	Cook Time: 45 minutes

Ingredients:

- 1 cup uncooked quinoa
- 2 cups vegetable broth or water
- 1 red bell pepper, chopped
- 1 zucchini, chopped
- 1 yellow squash, chopped
- 1 red onion, chopped
- 1 cup cherry tomatoes, halved
- 3 tbsp olive oil
- 2 tsp balsamic vinegar
- Salt and pepper to taste
- 1/4 cup fresh basil, chopped
- 1/4 cup fresh parsley, chopped
- 1 lemon, zested and juiced
- Optional toppings: sliced avocado, toasted pumpkin seeds, or crumbled feta (omit for vegan)

Directions:

1. Set oven temperature to 400°F or 200°C.

2. Toss olive oil, balsamic vinegar, salt, and pepper with red pepper, zucchini, yellow squash, red onion, and cherry tomatoes on a large baking sheet.

3. When the vegetables are soft and beginning to caramelise, roast them in a warm oven for 25 to 30 minutes, tossing them halfway through.

4. While the veggies are roasting, rinse the quinoa under cold water until the water runs clear.

5. In a pot, bring the water or vegetable broth to a boil. When the quinoa is cooked and the liquid has been absorbed, add it, lower the heat to low, cover it, and simmer for 15 minutes.

6. Take off the heat and use a fork to fluff. Let it sit covered for 5 minutes.

7. Mix the cooked quinoa with the roasted vegetables. Add fresh basil, parsley, lemon zest, and lemon juice. Toss to combine.

8. Serve warm, topped with optional toppings if desired.

Nutrition Information:

Calories: 600, **Carbohydrates:** 90g, **Protein:** 16g, **Fat:** 20g, **Sugar:** 9g, **Sodium:** 200mg, **Fiber:** 10g.

Chickpea and Kale Stir Fry

🕐 Time: 30 minutes	🍛 Serving Size: 4 servings
🥗 Prep Time: 10 minutes	👨‍🍳 Cook Time: 20 minutes

Ingredients:

• 2 cups cooked chickpeas (canned or cooked from dried)

• 4 cups kale, washed, stems removed, and chopped

• 2 tbsp olive oil

• 4 garlic cloves, minced

• 1 medium-sized red onion, thinly sliced

• 1 red bell pepper, cut into strips

• 2 tbsp low-sodium soy sauce or tamari (for a gluten-free option)

• 1 tbsp toasted sesame oil

• 1 tbsp apple cider vinegar

• 1 tsp ground black pepper

• Optional: 1 tsp red pepper flakes (for added heat)

• 2 tbsp sesame seeds (for garnish)

• 2 green onions, chopped (for garnish)

Directions:

1. In a big wok or skillet, heat the olive oil over medium-high heat.

2. Add the red onion slices, minced garlic, and sauté for about two minutes or until the onion turns translucent.

3. Stir in the red bell pepper slices and cook for 3 minutes.

4. Stir-fry the chickpeas in the skillet for around five minutes or until they begin to take on a golden brown color.

5. Toss in the chopped kale and stir-fry for another 2-3 minutes or until the kale is slightly wilted.

6. Mix the apple cider vinegar, sesame oil, ground black pepper, soy sauce or tamari, and optional red pepper flakes in a small bowl. Pour this mixture over the stir-fry and toss everything to combine.

7. Add 2 more minutes of cooking to allow the flavors to mingle.

8. Remove from heat and serve hot. As a garnish, add some chopped green onions and sesame seeds.

Nutrition Information:

Calories: 920, **Carbohydrates:** 122g, **Protein:** 38g, **Fat:** 32g, **Sugar:** 20g, **Sodium:** 800mg, **Fiber:** 28g.

Barley and Mushroom Risotto

🕐 Time: 50 minutes	🍛 Serving Size: 4 servings
🥗 Prep Time: 15 minutes	👨‍🍳 Cook Time: 35 minutes

Ingredients:

• 1 cup pearl barley, rinsed

• 4 cups vegetable

broth

• 2 tablespoons olive oil

• 1 small onion, finely

chopped

• 2 cloves garlic, minced

• 250g (8 oz) fresh mushrooms, sliced (shiitake, cremini, or portobello)

• 1/4 cup dry white wine (optional)

• 2 tablespoons fresh parsley, chopped

• Youcan add 1/4 cup of vegan parmesan or nutritional yeast. for extra flavor and creaminess

• Salt and pepper to taste

Directions:

1. In a large saucepan set over medium heat, cook the olive oil until it is fragrant.

2. Add the onion and sauté until translucent, about 2-3 minutes.

3. When the mushrooms and garlic have released their juices, simmer for a further five minutes.

4. If using white wine, add it now and let it decrease for about two minutes.

5. Stir in the barley, ensuring it's well-coated with the oil and veggies.

6. One cup of vegetable broth at a time; gradually add it while stirring continuously and letting the liquid permeate before adding more.

7. Continue to cook, stirring frequently, until the barley is tender and creamy. This will take about 30 minutes.

8. Once the barley is cooked and has a creamy consistency, stir in the nutritional yeast or vegan parmesan (if using) and fresh parsley— season with salt and pepper to taste.

9. Serve immediately, garnishing with additional parsley if desired.

Nutrition Information:

Calories: 290, **Carbohydrates:** 55g, **Protein:** 9g, **Fat:** 6g, **Sugar:** 3g, **Sodium:** 600mg, **Fiber:** 11g.

Bean and Vegetable Enchiladas

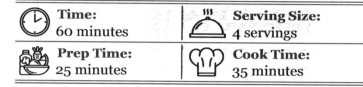

Time: 60 minutes		Serving Size: 4 servings	
Prep Time: 25 minutes		Cook Time: 35 minutes	

Ingredients:

• 12 whole grain or corn tortillas

• Two cups of cooked, drained, and rinsed pinto or black beans

• 1 cup corn kernels (fresh or frozen)

• 1 bell pepper, diced

• 1 zucchini, diced

• 1 onion, finely chopped

• 2 cloves garlic, minced

• 2 cups enchilada sauce (store-bought or homemade)

• 1 cup shredded vegan cheese (optional)

• 1 tablespoon olive oil

• Salt and pepper to taste

• Fresh cilantro and green onions for garnish

Directions:

1. Turn the oven on to 375°F, or 190°C.

2. In a big skillet, the olive oil needs to be heated over medium heat. Saute the bell pepper, onion, and zucchini for approximately five minutes or until tender.

3. Add the garlic and sauté for an additional minute until fragrant.

4. Add the corn and beans, season with salt and pepper, and simmer for two to three minutes. Remove from heat and set aside.

5. Fill a large baking dish with a thin coating of enchilada sauce.

6. To assemble the enchiladas:

7. Place a generous amount of the bean and vegetable mixture in the center of the tortilla.

8. Place the tortilla in the baking dish seam-side down after rolling it up.

9. Continue with the leftover tortillas.

10. Please make sure all rolled tortillas are coated by pouring the leftover enchilada sauce over them.

11. Sprinkle with vegan cheese if using.

12. Bake the baking dish for twenty-five minutes with the foil covering it. After removing the foil, bake for ten minutes or until the cheese is bubbling and melted.

13. Add fresh cilantro and sliced green onions as garnish just before serving.

Nutrition Information:

Calories: 325, **Carbohydrates:** 60g, **Protein:** 11g, **Fat:** 6g, **Sugar:** 6g, **Sodium:** 620mg, **Fiber:** 10g.

Couscous with Caramelized Onions and Almonds

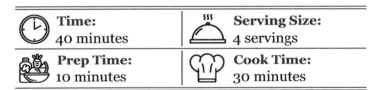

	Time: 40 minutes		Serving Size: 4 servings
	Prep Time: 10 minutes		Cook Time: 30 minutes

Ingredients:

- 1 cup whole wheat couscous
- 2 large onions, thinly sliced
- 1/3 cup almonds, coarsely chopped
- 2 tablespoons olive oil
- 1/4 teaspoon ground cinnamon
- 1/4 teaspoon ground cumin
- 2 cups low-sodium vegetable broth
- Salt and pepper to taste
- Fresh parsley, finely chopped for garnish

Directions:

1. Heat one tablespoon of olive oil in a big skillet over medium heat. Add a dash of salt and the onions. Simmer the onions for 20 to 25 minutes, stirring now and then, or until they are well caramelized and browned.

2. While the onions are caramelizing, in a separate skillet, toast the chopped almonds over medium heat until golden and fragrant, stirring often. This should take about 3-4 minutes. Remove from heat and set aside.

3. Once the onions are caramelized, stir in the ground cinnamon and cumin, cooking for another 2 minutes.

4. Heat the vegetable broth in a medium-sized pot until it begins to boil. Remove from heat, cover, and stir in the couscous. Let it sit for 5 minutes, then fluff it with a fork.

5. Move the couscous to a generously sized mixing bowl. Fold in the caramelized onions and toasted almonds. Garnish with freshly chopped parsley and serve in separate bowls.

6. Garnish with freshly chopped parsley and serve in separate bowls.

Nutrition Information:

Calories: 265, **Carbohydrates:** 42g, **Protein:** 8g, **Fat:** 8g, **Sugar:** 4g, **Sodium:** 130mg, **Fiber:** 6g.

Mung Bean and Spinach Soup

	Time: 50 minutes		Serving Size: 4 servings
	Prep Time: 10 minutes		Cook Time: 40 minutes

Ingredients:

- One cup of dried mung beans, soaked and drained the next day
- 4 cups low-sodium vegetable broth
- 2 cups fresh spinach, roughly chopped
- 1 medium onion, finely chopped
- 2 cloves garlic, minced
- 1 tablespoon olive oil
- 1/2 teaspoon ground turmeric
- 1/2 teaspoon ground cumin
- Salt and pepper to taste
- 1 tablespoon fresh lemon juice
- Fresh coriander (cilantro) for garnish

Directions:

1. The olive oil should be heated over medium heat in a large pot. Add the chopped onion and garlic, sautéing until translucent and fragrant, about 3-4 minutes.

2. Stir in the ground turmeric and cumin, cooking for an additional minute.

3. Add the soaked mung beans to the pot, stirring well to coat them in the onion and spices mixture.

4. After adding the veggie broth, heat the mixture until it boils. After turning the heat low, cover and cook the mung beans until they are soft, about 30 minutes.

5. Add the chopped spinach to the pot with the cooked mung beans. Cook for another 3-4 minutes or until the spinach has wilted.

6. Add salt, pepper, and freshly squeezed lemon juice to the soup. Stir well.

7. Serve hot in individual bowls, garnished with fresh coriander (cilantro).

Nutrition Information:

Calories: 190, **Carbohydrates:** 32g, **Protein:** 12g, **Fat:** 3g, **Sugar:** 3g, **Sodium:** 150mg, **Fiber:** 8g.

Lentil and Roasted Beet Salad

Time: 60 minutes	Serving Size: 4 servings
Prep Time: 15 minutes	Cook Time: 45 minutes

Ingredients:

- One cup of washed and drained dried green lentils
- 3 medium beets, trimmed, peeled, and cut into wedges
- 4 cups arugula
- 1/4 cup of feta cheese crumbles (for dairy-intolerant people only)
- 3 tablespoons olive oil, divided
- 2 tablespoons balsamic vinegar
- 1 clove garlic, minced
- Salt and pepper to taste
- 1/4 cup toasted walnuts, roughly chopped
- Fresh parsley for garnish

Directions:

1. Set oven temperature to 400°F or 200°C.

2. Toss beet wedges with 1 tablespoon of olive oil, salt, and pepper. Place them on a lined baking sheet and roast for 35-40 minutes or until tender and slightly caramelized.

3. In the meantime, boil three cups of water in a kettle. Along with a dash of salt, add the lentils. The lentils should be soft but not mushy after 25 to 30 minutes of simmering on low heat. Drain any excess water.

4. Whisk together the remaining 2 tablespoons of olive oil, balsamic vinegar, minced garlic, salt, and pepper in a small bowl to create the dressing.

5. The cooked lentils, arugula, dressing, and roasted beets should all be combined in a big mixing dish. Toss gently until everything is well combined.

6. Divide the salad among serving plates—

top with crumbled feta (if using), toasted walnuts, and fresh parsley.

Nutrition Information:

Calories: 280, **Carbohydrates:** 35g, **Protein:** 12g, **Fat:** 11g, **Sugar:** 8g, **Sodium:** 90mg, **Fiber:** 12g.

Chickpea and Veggie Burger Patties

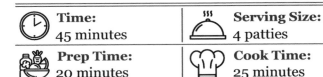

	Time: 45 minutes		Serving Size: 4 patties
	Prep Time: 20 minutes		Cook Time: 25 minutes

Ingredients:

• One can (15 oz) of rinsed and drained chickpeas

• 1/2 cup breadcrumbs (whole grain preferred)

• 1/2 onion, finely chopped

• 1 bell pepper (any color), finely chopped

• 1 carrot, grated

• 2 cloves garlic, minced

• 1 tablespoon olive oil

• 2 tablespoons tahini

or unsalted natural peanut butter

• 1 tablespoon soy sauce or tamari (low-sodium)

• 1 teaspoon smoked paprika

• 1/2 teaspoon ground cumin

• Salt and black pepper to taste

• 2 tablespoons fresh cilantro or parsley, chopped

Directions:

1. Combine chickpeas, breadcrumbs, tahini, soy sauce, smoked paprika, cumin, salt, and pepper in a food processor.Blend until the mixture largely becomes smooth and comes together.

2. After transferring the chickpea mixture to a mixing bowl, include the fresh herbs, bell pepper, onion, carrot, and garlic.

3. Form the mixture into 4 equal-sized patties.

4. Olive oil should be heated in a skillet that does not adhere to the hob over medium heat. After adding the patties to the skillet, fry them for 10 to 12 minutes on each side or until they are crispy and golden brown.

5. Remove from the heat and serve with your choice of whole grain bun, lettuce, tomato, and any preferred condiments.

Nutrition Information:

Calories: 260, **Carbohydrates:** 39g, **Protein:** 10g, **Fat:** 8g, **Sugar:** 6g, **Sodium:** 320mg, **Fiber:** 9g.

Chapter 8: Soups

Tomato Basil Soup with Chia Seeds

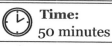 Time: 50 minutes	Serving Size: 4 servings
Prep Time: 10 minutes	Cook Time: 40 minutes

Ingredients:

- 6 ripe tomatoes, diced
- 1 onion, finely chopped
- 3 cloves garlic, minced
- 2 tablespoons olive oil
- 4 cups low-sodium vegetable broth
- 1/4 cup fresh basil leaves, chopped
- 2 tablespoons chia seeds
- 1 teaspoon dried oregano
- Salt and pepper to taste
- 1/4 cup low-fat cream (optional for creaminess)
- 1 tablespoon balsamic vinegar (optional for added depth)

Directions:

1. Pour olive oil into a big pot and warm it up to medium. Add the chopped onion and sauté until translucent, about 3-4 minutes.

2. For a further one to two minutes, add the minced garlic and sauté.

3. Stir in the diced tomatoes, oregano, salt, and pepper. Cook for about 10 minutes, allowing the tomatoes to release their juices.

4. After adding the veggie broth, heat the mixture until it boils. After lowering the heat to low, cover and simmer for twenty minutes.

5. Once the soup has simmered, purée it until smooth using a hand blender or a stand blender in stages.

6. Put the soup back in the saucepan if you're using a stand blender. Stir in the chopped basil, chia seeds, and low-fat cream. Allow to simmer for another 5 minutes.

7. If desired, stir in balsamic vinegar for added depth in flavor.

8. Serve hot, garnished with additional basil or a sprinkle of chia seeds on top.

Nutrition Information:

Calories: 160, **Carbohydrates:** 21g, **Protein:** 4g, **Fat:** 7g, **Sugar:** 8g, **Sodium:** 130mg, **Fiber:** 5g.

Butternut Squash and Ginger Soup

Time: 1 hour	Serving Size: 6 servings
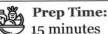 Prep Time: 15 minutes	Cook Time: 45 minutes

Ingredients:

- 1 medium butternut squash (about four cups), peeled and cubed
- 1 onion, chopped
- 2 tablespoons fresh ginger, minced
- 2 cloves garlic, minced
- 4 cups low-sodium vegetable broth
- 1 can (14 oz) light coconut milk
- 1 tablespoon olive oil
- 1 teaspoon ground turmeric
- Salt and pepper to taste
- Fresh cilantro or parsley for garnish (optional)

Directions:

1. The olive oil should be warmed over medium heat in a big pot. Add the chopped onion and sauté until translucent, about 4 minutes.

2. Add the minced ginger and garlic. Continue to sauté for another 2 minutes.

3. Stir in the butternut squash cubes, ensuring they're coated in the onion, ginger, and garlic mixture.

4. After adding the veggie broth, heat the mixture until it boils. Once boiling, reduce the heat, cover, and let it simmer for about 25-30 minutes or until the squash is tender.

5. After the squash is tender, remove from the heat and use a hand blender or a stand mixer in stages to puree the soup until it's smooth.

6. If you use a stand blender, transfer the soup to the pot and blend in the ground turmeric and coconut milk—season with salt and pepper to taste.

7. Heat the soup on low for another 10 minutes until it's heated.

8. If preferred, top with freshly chopped parsley or cilantro and serve hot.

Nutrition Information:

Calories: 140, **Carbohydrates:** 25g, **Protein:** 2g, **Fat:** 4g, **Sugar:** 5g, **Sodium:** 120mg, **Fiber:** 4g.

Spiced Lentil and Vegetable Soup

Time: 1 hour 15 minutes	Serving Size: 6servings
Prep Time: 15 minutes	Cook Time: 1 hour

Ingredients:

- One cup of washed and drained dried green lentils
- 4 cups low-sodium vegetable broth
- 2 cups water
- 1 medium onion, chopped
- 2 carrots, diced
- 2 celery stalks, diced
- 3 garlic cloves, minced
- 1 medium zucchini, chopped
- One can (14.5 oz) of chopped tomatoes without salt added
- 1 tablespoon olive oil
- 1 teaspoon ground cumin
- 1/2 teaspoon ground turmeric
- 1/2 teaspoon smoked paprika
- Salt and pepper to taste
- Fresh parsley or cilantro for garnish (optional)

Directions:

1. Heat the olive oil in a big pot over medium heat. Add the chopped onion, diced carrots, and celery. Sauté until the onion becomes translucent, about 5 minutes.

2. Add the minced garlic and sauté for an additional two minutes when aromatic.

3. Stir in the lentils, ensuring they are well-coated with the sautéed vegetables.

4. Add the vegetable broth, water, diced tomatoes, zucchini, ground cumin, turmeric, and smoked paprika. Stir well.

5. Bring the mixture to a boil. When the lentils are tender, around 50 to 55 minutes of simmering time is required; once boiling, lower the heat and cover.

6. Season with salt and pepper to taste.

7. If preferred, top with chopped cilantro or fresh parsley and serve hot.

Nutrition Information:

Calories: 160, **Carbohydrates:** 28g, **Protein:** 8g, **Fat:** 2.5g, **Sugar:** 5g, **Sodium:** 135mg, **Fiber:** 7g.

Chicken Noodle Soup with Zucchini Noodles

🕐 Time: 1 hour	🍽 Serving Size: 4 servings
🥗 Prep Time: 15 minutes	👨‍🍳 Cook Time: 45 minutes

Ingredients:

- 2 medium-sized chicken breasts, skinless and boneless
- 4 cups low-sodium chicken broth
- 2 medium zucchinis, spiralized into noodles
- 1 medium onion, chopped
- 2 carrots, sliced
- 2 celery stalks, sliced
- 3 garlic cloves, minced
- 1 tablespoon olive oil
- 1 bay leaf
- 1 teaspoon dried thyme
- Salt and pepper to taste
- 2 tablespoons fresh parsley, chopped
- 1 lemon, zested and juiced

Directions:

1. In a large pot, preheat the olive oil over medium heat. Add the chopped onion, sliced carrots, and celery. Sauté until the onion becomes translucent, about 5 minutes.

2. For a further one to two minutes, add the minced garlic and sauté.

3. Place the chicken breasts in the pot and pour in the chicken broth, ensuring the chicken is submerged.

4. Add the bay leaf, dried thyme, salt, and pepper.

5. Simmer the mixture after bringing it to a boil. Cover and let it simmer for 25-30 minutes or until the chicken is cooked.

6. Taking out of the pot, shred the chicken breasts with two forks.

7. Return the shredded chicken to the pot.

8. Add the zucchini noodles to the soup and cook for 5 minutes or until the zucchini noodles are tender but not overly soft.

9. Remove the bay leaf. Before serving, stir in the lemon zest, juice, and fresh parsley.

Nutrition Information:

Calories: 165, **Carbohydrates:** 11g, **Protein:** 19g, **Fat:** 5g, **Sugar:** 5g, **Sodium:** 150mg, **Fiber:** 3g.

Creamy Broccoli Soup (dairy-free)

🕐 Time: 45 minutes	🍽 Serving Size: 4 servings
🥗 Prep Time: 15 minutes	👨‍🍳 Cook Time: 30 minutes

Ingredients:

- 4 cups broccoli florets (about 2 medium heads of broccoli)
- 1 large onion, diced
- 2 garlic cloves, minced

- 4 cups vegetable broth (low-sodium)
- 1 cup canned coconut milk (full-fat)
- 1 tablespoon olive oil
- 1/2 teaspoon salt (adjust based on preference and broth sodium content)
- 1/4 teaspoon black pepper
- 1/4 teaspoon nutmeg
- 1 tablespoon nutritional yeast (optional for a cheesy flavor)
- 1 tablespoon fresh lemon juice

Directions:

1. In a large pot, preheat the olive oil over medium heat. Add diced onion and sauté until translucent, about 5 minutes.

2. Add minced garlic and continue sautéing for another 2 minutes.

3. Add broccoli florets to the pot and stir well. Cook for another 3-4 minutes until the broccoli turns a bright green.

4. After adding the veggie broth, heat the mixture until it boils. Once the broccoli is cooked, reduce heat, cover, and simmer for about 20 minutes.

5. Turn off the heat and blend the soup using an immersion blender until smooth. Use a conventional blender in batches to carefully transfer the soup and blend it until smooth if you don't have an immersion blender. Reintroduce the pureed soup into the saucepan. Stir in coconut milk, salt, black pepper, nutmeg, and nutritional yeast (if using). Heat over low heat until warmed through.

6. Add the freshly squeezed lemon juice right before serving. Adjust seasoning if necessary.

Nutrition Information:

Calories: 190, **Carbohydrates:** 18g, **Protein:** 6g, **Fat:** 13g, **Sugar:** 5g, **Sodium:** 500mg, **Fiber:** 5g.

Seafood Chowder with Cauliflower Cream

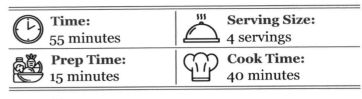

	Time: 55 minutes		Serving Size: 4 servings
	Prep Time: 15 minutes		Cook Time: 40 minutes

Ingredients:

- 1 medium cauliflower head, cut into florets
- 2 cups vegetable or seafood broth (low-sodium)
- 8 oz shrimp, peeled and deveined
- 8 oz scallops
- 4 oz clams, cleaned
- 1 medium onion, diced
- 2 garlic cloves, minced
- 1 tablespoon olive oil
- 1/2 cup celery, diced
- 1/4 cup fresh parsley, chopped
- 1 teaspoon dried thyme
- Salt and pepper to taste
- 1 cup unsweetened almond milk
- 1 tablespoon lemon juice

Directions:

1. Add the stock and cauliflower florets to a large pot. Reduce the heat and cook the cauliflower for about 20 minutes or until tender.

2. Blend the cauliflower with an immersion blender (or a conventional blender in batches) until it becomes a smooth and creamy texture.

3. This is your cauliflower cream.

4. Heat the olive oil in a large pot separate over medium heat. Add onions and celery and sauté until translucent, about 5 minutes.

5. Add minced garlic and sauté for another minute.

6. Add shrimp, scallops, and clams to the pot. Cook for 5-7 minutes, stirring occasionally until the seafood is almost cooked.

7. Add the cauliflower cream, almond milk, dried thyme, parsley, lemon juice, salt, and pepper. Stir well to combine.

8. Bring the mixture to a gentle simmer and let it cook for an additional 10 minutes.

9. Before serving, check the seasoning and make any required adjustments.

Nutrition Information:

Calories: 210, **Carbohydrates:** 15g, **Protein:** 24g, **Fat:** 6g, **Sugar:** 5g, **Sodium:** 450mg, **Fiber:** 4g.

Vegan Tuscan White Bean Soup

⏰ Time: 50 minutes	🍽 Serving Size: 6 servings
🥗 Prep Time: 10 minutes	👨‍🍳 Cook Time: 40 minutes

Ingredients:

- 2 tablespoons olive oil
- 1 large onion, chopped
- 3 garlic cloves, minced
- 2 carrots, diced
- 2 celery stalks, diced
- 4 cups vegetable broth (low-sodium)
- Two fifteen-ounce cans of washed and drained white beans (cannellini or navy beans)
- One 14.5-oz can of chopped tomatoes without added salt
- 2 teaspoons dried Italian herbs (or a mix of dried oregano, basil, and thyme)
- 1 bay leaf
- 4 cups fresh kale, de-stemmed and roughly chopped
- Salt and pepper to taste
- Juice of half a lemon
- Fresh parsley, for garnish (optional)

Directions:

1. Pour olive oil into a big pot and warm it up to medium. Add onions, carrots, and celery. Sauté until onions are translucent, about 5 minutes.

2. Add garlic and sauté for another minute.

3. Pour in vegetable broth, white beans, and diced tomatoes (with their juice). Stir to combine.

4. Add dried Italian herbs, bay leaf, salt, and pepper. Bring the soup to a boil.

5. After it boils, lower the heat to a simmer for twenty-five minutes.

6. After simmering, add in the chopped kale. Simmer for another 5-10 minutes or until kale is tender.

7. Remove the bay leaf, add lemon juice, and adjust salt and pepper to taste.

8. If preferred, top a hot dish with fresh parsley.

Nutrition Information:

Calories: 200, **Carbohydrates:** 34g, **Protein:** 11g, **Fat:** 3g, **Sugar:** 4g, **Sodium:** 200mg, **Fiber:** 9g.

Beef and Vegetable Barley Soup

⏰ Time: 1 hour 45 minutes	🍽 Serving Size: 6 servings
🥗 Prep Time: 15 minutes	👨‍🍳 Cook Time: 1 hour 30 minutes

Ingredients:

- 1 pound lean beef stew meat, cubed
- 1 tablespoon olive oil
- 1 onion, chopped
- 2 garlic cloves, minced
- 3 carrots, peeled and sliced
- 2 celery stalks, chopped
- 3/4 cup pearl barley, rinsed
- 6 cups beef broth (low-sodium)
- One 14.5-oz can of chopped tomatoes without added salt
- 2 bay leaves

- 1 teaspoon dried thyme
- Salt and pepper to taste
- 2 cups chopped green

beans
- 2 cups chopped zucchini
- Fresh parsley, for garnish (optional)

Directions:

1. Olive oil should be heated in a large saucepan over medium-high heat. Brown the beef cubes on all sides after adding them. Remove beef and set aside.

2. Celery, carrots, and onions should all be added to the same pot. Sauté until onions are translucent, about 5 minutes.

3. Add garlic and sauté for another minute.

4. Return the beef to the pot, and add barley, broth, diced tomatoes, bay leaves, dried thyme, salt, and pepper.

5. Once the mixture is to a boil, lower the heat, cover it, and simmer the stew until the barley and beef are soft about 1 hour.

6. Add the green beans and zucchini to the pot and cook for 15-20 minutes until the vegetables are tender.

7. Remove the bay leaves. Adjust the seasoning if necessary.

8. If preferred, top a hot dish with fresh parsley.

Nutrition Information:

Calories: 280, **Carbohydrates:** 33g, **Protein:** 25g, **Fat:** 5g, **Sugar:** 6g, **Sodium:** 250mg, **Fiber:** 8g.

Cold Cucumber and Dill Soup

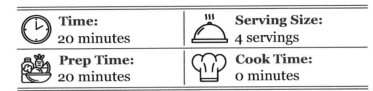

	Time: 20 minutes		Serving Size: 4 servings
	Prep Time: 20 minutes		Cook Time: 0 minutes

Ingredients:

- 4 medium-sized cucumbers, peeled, seeded, and roughly chopped
- 2 cups unsweetened plain yogurt (preferably Greek yogurt for thicker consistency)
- 2 tablespoons fresh dill, finely chopped, plus extra for garnish
- 1 garlic clove, minced
- 1 tablespoon olive oil
- 1 tablespoon lemon juice
- Salt and pepper to taste
- 1/4 cup cold water (or as needed to achieve desired consistency)
- Fresh dill sprigs for garnish

Directions:

1. Add the yogurt, dill, garlic, olive oil, lemon juice, and cucumbers to a food processor or blender. Mix until homogeneous.

2. Add cold water until the soup reaches the right consistency if it's too thick.

3. Season with salt and pepper to taste.

4. To enable the flavors to mingle, transfer the soup into a bowl, cover it, and place it in the refrigerator for at least two hours before serving.

5. Serve cold, garnished with fresh dill sprigs.

Nutrition Information:

Calories: 120, **Carbohydrates:** 11g, **Protein:** 6g, **Fat:** 6g, **Sugar:** 7g, **Sodium:** 45mg, **Fiber:** 1g

Spicy Tomato and Bean Soup

Time: 45 minutes	**Serving Size:** 6 servings
Prep Time: 15 minutes	**Cook Time:** 30 minutes

Nutrition Information:

Calories: 190, **Carbohydrates:** 35g, **Protein:** 10g, **Fat:** 3g, **Sugar:** 5g, **Sodium:** 420mg, **Fiber:** 10g.

Ingredients:

- 1 tablespoon olive oil
- 1 medium onion, finely chopped
- 3 garlic cloves, minced
- 1 jalapeño pepper, seeds removed and finely chopped (adjust based on heat preference)
- 2 cans (14.5 ounces each) of diced tomatoes, undrained
- One fifteen-ounce can of rinsed and drained black beans
- 1 can (15 ounces) kidney beans, drained and rinsed
- 4 cups low-sodium vegetable broth
- 1 teaspoon ground cumin
- 1/2 teaspoon smoked paprika
- Salt and pepper to taste
- Fresh cilantro for garnish
- 1 lime, cut into wedges

Directions:

1. In a big pot set over medium heat, warm the olive oil. Add the onion and sauté until translucent, about 5 minutes.

2. Add the garlic and jalapeño, and sauté for another 2 minutes until fragrant.

3. Stir in the diced tomatoes, black beans, kidney beans, vegetable broth, cumin, and smoked paprika. Bring to a boil.

4. Let the flavors melt together by lowering the heat and simmering for 25 to 30 minutes.

5. Season with salt and pepper to taste.

6. Serve hot with a wedge of lime and some fresh cilantro.

Chapter 9: Snacks and Sides

Baked Zucchini Fries

Time: 30 minutes	**Serving Size:** 4 servings
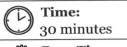 **Prep Time:** 10 minutes	**Cook Time:** 20 minutes

Ingredients:

- 2 medium zucchinis
- Half a cup almond flour (for a non-gluten-free option, use whole wheat breadcrumbs)
- 1/4 cup grated Parmesan cheese (use nutritional yeast for a dairy-free version)
- 1 teaspoon dried oregano
- 1 teaspoon garlic powder
- Salt and pepper to taste
- 1 egg, beaten
- Cooking spray or olive oil for light brushing

Directions:

1. Pinch the oven's temperature to 425°F (220°C), then line a baking pan with parchment paper.

2. Cut the zucchini into fry-like strips, approximately 3-4 inches long.

3. Mix almond flour, Parmesan cheese or nutritional yeast, oregano, garlic powder, salt, and pepper in a small bowl.

4. Dip each zucchini strip into the beaten egg, ensuring it's well coated, and then dredge in the almond flour mixture. Make sure each strip is covered well.

5. Place the coated zucchini strips on the prepared baking sheet, ensuring they're not touching each other.

6. Apply a thin frying spray or lightly brush the zucchini fries with olive oil.

7. Bake for about 20 minutes at around 200 degrees until crisp and golden.

8. Let cool somewhat before arranging to serve.

Nutrition Information:

Calories: 120, **Carbohydrates:** 7g, **Protein:** 6g, **Fat:** 8g, **Sugar:** 2g, **Sodium:** 140mg, **Fiber:** 3g.

Stuffed Mini Bell Peppers

Time: 30 minutes	**Serving Size:** 4 servings
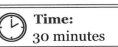 **Prep Time:** 10 minutes	**Cook Time:** 20 minutes

Ingredients:

- 12 mini bell peppers
- 1 cup cooked quinoa
- Half a cup of rinsed and drained black beans

- 1/4 cup fresh corn kernels
- 1/4 cup finely diced red onion
- 1/2 avocado, finely diced
- 1/4 cup fresh cilantro, chopped
- 1 teaspoon cumin powder
- Salt and pepper to taste
- Juice of 1 lime
- 1 tablespoon olive oil

Directions:

1. Turn the oven on to 375°F, or 190°C.

2. Cut off the tops of the mini bell peppers and remove the seeds.

3. Combine quinoa, black beans, corn, red onion, avocado, cilantro, cumin, salt, pepper, and lime juice in a mixing bowl. Mix well until all ingredients are well combined.

4. Carefully stuff each mini bell pepper with the quinoa mixture.

5. Spread some olive oil on a baking dish and arrange the filled peppers.

6. Bake the peppers for 20 minutes or until they are soft and beginning to turn brown.

7. Serve warm and enjoy!

Nutrition Information:

Calories: 180, **Carbohydrates:** 27g, **Protein:** 6g, **Fat:** 6g, **Sugar:** 5g, **Sodium:** 60mg, **Fiber:** 7g.

15-ounce can, rinsed and drained)
- 1 tablespoon olive oil
- 1 teaspoon smoked paprika
- 1/2 teaspoon cayenne pepper (adjust based on

desired spiciness)
- 1/2 teaspoon garlic powder
- 1/4 teaspoon ground black pepper
- 1/2 teaspoon sea salt

Directions:

1. Set oven temperature to 400°F or 200°C.

2. Pat the chickpeas dry using a clean kitchen towel or paper towel. Remove any loose skins.

3. Chickpeas, olive oil, smoked paprika, cayenne, garlic powder, black pepper, and sea salt should all be combined in a mixing dish. Stir thoroughly to coat the chickpeas evenly.

4. Distribute the chickpeas in a uniform layer on a baking sheet covered with silicone baking mats or parchment paper.

5. Roast in the oven for 25-30 minutes, stirring them, or shake halfway through until crispy and golden brown.

6. Let them cool slightly before serving. When they cool, they will keep getting crispier.

Nutrition Information:

Calories: 140, **Carbohydrates:** 20g, **Protein:** 6g, **Fat:** 4g, **Sugar:** 3g, **Sodium:** 300mg, **Fiber:** 5g.

Spicy Roasted Chickpeas

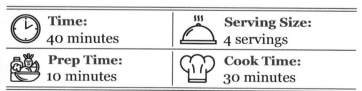

⏱ Time: 40 minutes	🍽 Serving Size: 4 servings
🥗 Prep Time: 10 minutes	👨‍🍳 Cook Time: 30 minutes

Ingredients:

- 2 cups of cooked   chickpeas (or one

Garlic Parmesan Green Bean Fries

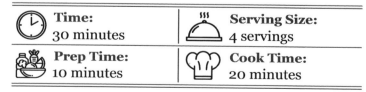

⏱ Time: 30 minutes	🍽 Serving Size: 4 servings
🥗 Prep Time: 10 minutes	👨‍🍳 Cook Time: 20 minutes

Ingredients:

- 1 pound fresh green   beans, trimmed

- 1 tablespoon olive oil
- 2 cloves garlic, finely minced
- 1/4 cup grated Parmesan cheese
- 1/2 teaspoon sea salt
- 1/4 teaspoon ground
- black pepper
- 1 teaspoon dried Italian seasoning (optional)
- 1/4 cup almond flour (for coating)

Directions:

1. Pinch the oven's temperature to 425°F (220°C), then line a baking pan with parchment paper.

2. Make sure the green beans are equally covered by tossing them in a big bowl of olive oil.

3. Add minced garlic, Parmesan cheese, sea salt, black pepper, and Italian seasoning (if using). Mix well.

4. Sprinkle the almond flour over the green beans and toss again, making sure the beans are lightly coated.

5. Spread the green beans on the prepared baking sheet in a single layer.

6. Bake, stirring halfway through to ensure equal cooking, for 18 to 20 minutes or until the beans are brown and slightly crispy.

7. Take them out of the oven and allow them to cool a little before serving.

Nutrition Information:

Calories: 120, **Carbohydrates:** 10g, **Protein:** 6g, **Fat:** 7g, **Sugar:** 3g, **Sodium:** 330mg, **Fiber:** 4g.

Sweet Potato and Rosemary Bites

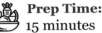 Time: 40 minutes	Serving Size: 6 servings
Prep Time: 15 minutes	Cook Time: 25 minutes

Ingredients:

- 2 medium sweet potatoes, chopped into 1-inch pieces after peeling.
- 2 tablespoons olive oil
- 1 tablespoon fresh rosemary, finely chopped
- 1/2 teaspoon sea salt
- 1/4 teaspoon freshly ground black pepper
- 1/4 teaspoon smoked paprika (optional)
- 1 tablespoon grated Parmesan cheese (optional for added flavor)

Directions:

1. As you prepare a baking sheet, preheat the oven to 425°F (220°C).

2. Combine the chopped sweet potatoes and olive oil in a sizable mixing bowl.

3. Sprinkle the rosemary, sea salt, black pepper, and smoked paprika (if using) over the sweet potatoes. To make sure they are coated equally, toss them thoroughly.

4. Place the cubed sweet potatoes in a single layer on the hot baking sheet.

5. Bake, tossing regularly to promote equal cooking, in a preheated oven for 20 to 25 minutes or until they are soft and lightly browned around the edges.

6. Before serving, top the baked sweet potato bits with grated Parmesan cheese for an extra flavorful layer.

Nutrition Information:

Calories: 105, **Carbohydrates:** 18g, **Protein:** 1g, **Fat:** 3.5g, **Sugar:** 3g, **Sodium:** 215mg, **Fiber:** 3g.

Cucumber and Avocado Rolls

 Time: 20 minutes

 Serving Size: 6 servings

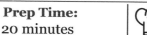 **Prep Time:** 20 minutes

Cook Time: 0 minutes

Ingredients:

- 1 large cucumber
- 2 ripe avocados, peeled and pitted
- 1 tablespoon lemon juice
- 1/4 teaspoon sea salt
- 1/4 teaspoon freshly ground black pepper
- 1 tablespoon fresh dill, chopped (optional)
- 1/4 teaspoon optionally crushed red pepper flakes for a bit of heat
- 1 tablespoon chia seeds (for added texture and nutrition, optional)

Directions:

1. Slice the cucumber lengthwise and thinly with a vegetable peeler.

2. In a mixing bowl, mash the avocados until relatively smooth.

3. Stir in the lemon juice, sea salt, black pepper, dill (if using), and red pepper flakes (if using) to the mashed avocado.

4. Lay the cucumber strips flat on a clean surface. Place a small amount of the avocado mixture at one end of each strip.

5. Roll the cucumber around the avocado mixture, creating a small roll.

6. If desired, sprinkle each roll lightly with chia seeds.

7. Serve immediately or put in the fridge until you're ready to eat.

Nutrition Information:

Calories: 100, **Carbohydrates:** 7g, **Protein:** 2g, **Fat:** 8g, **Sugar:** 1g, **Sodium:** 105mg, **Fiber:** 4g.

Cauliflower Tots with Dipping Sauce

 Time: 35 minutes

 Serving Size: 4 servings

 Prep Time: 15 minutes

 Cook Time: 20 minutes

Ingredients:

- **For the Cauliflower Tots:**
- 1 medium-sized cauliflower head that has been chopped into florets
- 1/4 cup almond flour or breadcrumbs (for a gluten-free option, use almond flour)
- 1/4 cup grated Parmesan cheese
- 1 egg, beaten
- 1/2 teaspoon garlic powder
- 1/2 teaspoon onion powder
- Salt and pepper to taste
- Olive oil or cooking spray for greasing
- **For the Dipping Sauce:**
- 1/4 cup Greek yogurt (use unsweetened for diabetic-friendly)
- 1 tablespoon lemon juice
- 1 tablespoon fresh chives, chopped
- Salt and pepper to taste

Directions:

1. Set oven temperature to 400°F or 200°C. Apply cooking spray or olive oil sparingly to a baking sheet.

2. Steam the cauliflower florets until they're tender, about 5-7 minutes. Let them cool slightly.

3. Grate the steamed cauliflower finely in a food processor by pulsing it.

4. Transfer the grated cauliflower to a large mixing bowl. Add the beaten egg, grated Parmesan cheese, garlic and onion powders, salt, and pepper, along with the almond flour or breadcrumbs. Stir until thoroughly mixed.

5. Place the mixture into tiny, cylindrical tots on the prepared baking sheet.

6. Bake the tots for 20 minutes or until crispy and golden brown.

7. While the tots are baking, prepare the dipping sauce. Mix Greek yogurt, lemon juice, chives, salt, and pepper in a small bowl.

8. Serve the cauliflower tots hot with the dipping sauce on the side.

Nutrition Information:

Calories: 125, **Carbohydrates:** 10g, **Protein:** 8g, **Fat:** 6g, **Sugar:** 3g, **Sodium:** 220mg, **Fiber:** 3g.

4. Bake in the oven for 10 minutes or until the asparagus is tender and the prosciutto is crisp.

5. Take out of the oven, and while still warm, top with grated Parmesan cheese if preferred.

6. Serve immediately.

Nutrition Information:

Calories: 90, **Carbohydrates:** 3g, **Protein:** 7g, **Fat:** 6g, **Sugar:** 1g, **Sodium:** 620mg, **Fiber:** 1g.

Asparagus Wrapped in Prosciutto

🕐 **Time:** 20 minutes	ᗰ **Serving Size:** 4 servings
🥗 **Prep Time:** 10 minutes	👨‍🍳 **Cook Time:** 10 minutes

Ingredients:

- 16 fresh asparagus spears, trimmed
- 8 slices of prosciutto, halved lengthwise
- 1 tablespoon olive oil
- 1/4 teaspoon freshly ground black pepper
- 1 tablespoon grated Parmesan cheese (optional)
- Zest of 1 lemon (optional for added flavor)

Directions:

1. Set the oven temperature to 425°F (220°C).

2. Lay the half-slice of prosciutto on a flat surface. Place an asparagus spear at one end of the prosciutto slice and roll it up. Continue with the remaining pieces of prosciutto and asparagus spears.

3. Placed on a baking sheet, arrange the wrapped asparagus. After drizzling with olive oil, season with black pepper. If desired, sprinkle with lemon zest for added flavor.

Baked Spinach and Cheese Stuffed Mushrooms

🕐 **Time:** 30 minutes	ᗰ **Serving Size:** 4 servings
🥗 **Prep Time:** 10 minutes	👨‍🍳 **Cook Time:** 20 minutes

Ingredients:

- 8 large button mushrooms, stems removed and finely chopped (set caps aside)
- 2 cups fresh spinach, finely chopped
- 1/2 cup grated mozzarella cheese
- 1/4 cup grated Parmesan cheese
- 1 tablespoon olive oil
- 2 cloves garlic, minced
- 1/4 teaspoon black pepper
- 1/4 teaspoon of optionally spicy red pepper flakes
- 1/4 teaspoon salt

Directions:

1. Turn the oven on to 375°F, or 190°C.

2. Warm up the olive oil in a medium-sized skillet over medium heat. Saute the garlic for one minute after adding it.

3. Cook the finely chopped mushroom stems in the skillet for three to four minutes or until they release their liquid.

4. After adding the spinach, simmer for two more minutes or until it wilts.

5. Take off the heat and mix the red pepper flakes, black pepper, half of the Parmesan cheese, and mozzarella cheese.

6. Press down to ensure the spinach and cheese mixture is fully inserted into each mushroom cap.

7. After placing the filled mushrooms on a baking sheet, cover them with the leftover Parmesan cheese.

8. Bake in a preheated oven for about 20 minutes or until the mushrooms are soft and the caps are browned.

9. Take them out of the oven, let them cool down for a little while, and then serve hot.

Nutrition Information:

Calories: 125, **Carbohydrates:** 6g, **Protein:** 9g, **Fat:** 8g, **Sugar:** 2g, **Sodium:** 350mg, **Fiber:** 2g.

Directions:

1. Combine diced tomatoes, red onion, garlic, and fresh basil in a mixing bowl.

2. Mix the olive oil, balsamic vinegar, salt, black pepper, and red pepper flakes (if using) in another small bowl.

3. After adding the olive oil combination to the tomato mixture, gently toss to coat.

4. Let the tomato mixture sit for 10 minutes to marinate and meld the flavors.

5. Toast the whole-grain baguette slices until they're crisp and golden brown.

6. Place a substantial portion of the tomato mixture onto every slice of toasted bread.

7. Serve immediately and enjoy!

Nutrition Information:

Calories: 115, **Carbohydrates:** 20g, **Protein:** 4g, **Fat:** 3g, **Sugar:** 4g, **Sodium:** 260mg, **Fiber:** 3g.

Tangy Tomato Bruschetta

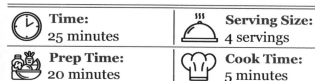

🕐 **Time:** 25 minutes	🍽 **Serving Size:** 4 servings
🥗 **Prep Time:** 20 minutes	👨‍🍳 **Cook Time:** 5 minutes

Ingredients:

- 8 slices of whole-grain baguette, toasted
- 2 large ripe tomatoes, finely diced
- 1/4 cup red onion, finely chopped
- 2 cloves garlic, minced
- 2 tablespoons fresh basil, chopped
- 1 tablespoon extra-virgin olive oil
- 1 tablespoon balsamic vinegar
- 1/4 teaspoon black pepper
- 1/4 teaspoon salt
- 1/4 teaspoon of optionally spicy red pepper flakes

Chapter 10: Dessert Delights

Dark Chocolate Avocado Mousse

Time: 15 minutes	**Serving Size:** 4 servings
Prep Time: 15 minutes	**Cook Time:** 0 minutes

Ingredients:

- 2 ripe avocados, pitted and scooped out
- 1/2 cup unsweetened dark cocoa powder
- 1/4 cup almond milk, unsweetened (or another milk alternative)
- 1/4 cup pure

maple syrup or stevia equivalent

- 1 tsp vanilla extract
- A pinch of sea salt
- 1/4 cup unsweetened dark chocolate chips (optional for garnish)
- Fresh berries (optional for garnish)

Directions:

1. Add ripe avocados, sea salt, almond milk, vanilla essence, and dark chocolate powder in a food processor or blender.

2. Blend until creamy and smooth, removing any lumps of avocado.

3. Taste the mousse and adjust sweetness, if necessary.

4. Transfer the mousse into individual serving bowls or glasses.

5. Refrigerate for at least an hour, allowing the mousse to set and flavors to intensify.

6. Before serving, garnish with dark chocolate chips and fresh berries, if desired.

7. Enjoy your creamy, guilt-free dessert!

Nutrition Information:

Calories: 220, **Carbohydrates:** 25g, **Protein:** 4g, **Fat:** 15g, **Sugar:** 10g, **Sodium:** 30mg, **Fiber:** 8g.

Berries and Cream Chia Pudding

Time: 4 hours 10 minutes	**Serving Size:** 4 servings
Prep Time: 10 minutes	**Cook Time:** 0 minutes

Ingredients:

- 1/4 cup chia seeds
- One cup of unsweetened almond milk (or another type of milk)
- 1 tsp vanilla extract
- 1-2 tbsp stevia or other diabetic-friendly

sweetener, adjusted to taste

- 1/2 cup mixed berries (like blueberries, strawberries, raspberries)
- 1/4 cup heavy cream (or, for a dairy-free option, coconut cream)

- Fresh mint leaves   (optional for garnish)

Directions:

1. Mix the sugar, almond milk, vanilla essence, and chia seeds in a bowl. Give it a good five minutes to sit.

2. Stir the mixture again to ensure no clumps, then divide among four serving glasses or bowls.

3. Cover and refrigerate for at least 4 hours or until the pudding has set.

4. Before serving, whip the heavy cream (or coconut cream) until soft peaks form.

5. Place a dollop of whipped cream and an equal amount of mixed berries on top of each chia pudding.

6. Garnish with fresh mint leaves if desired.

7. Serve and enjoy!

Nutrition Information:

Calories: 150, **Carbohydrates:** 10g, **Protein:** 4g, **Fat:** 11g, **Sugar:** 3g, **Sodium:** 40mg, **Fiber:** 6g.

Directions:

1. Process the almonds in a food processor until they resemble coarse flour.

2. Add the shredded coconut, chia seeds, melted coconut oil, sweetener, vanilla extract, and salt (and cocoa powder) to the food processor.

3. Blend until the mixture starts to come together. A little more coconut oil can be added if it looks too dry.

4. Roll the mixture into 12 uniformly sized balls with your hands.

5. Place the energy balls on a tray lined with parchment paper.

6. Chill in the refrigerator for at least 10 minutes to set.

7. After it sets, move it to a refrigerator-safe container and seal it.

8. Enjoy as a delightful and energizing snack!

Nutrition Information:

Calories: 120, **Carbohydrates:** 5g, **Protein:** 3g, **Fat:** 11g, **Sugar:** 1g, **Sodium:** 5mg, **Fiber:** 3g.

Almond and Coconut Energy Balls

⏱ Time: 30 minutes	🍽 Serving Size: 12 balls
🥗 Prep Time: 20 minutes	👨‍🍳 Cook Time: 10 minutes

Ingredients:

- 1 cup raw almonds
- 1/2 cup unsweetened shredded coconut
- 2 tbsp chia seeds
- 1/4 cup coconut oil, melted
- 1-2 tbsp stevia or another diabetic-friendly sweetener, adjusted to taste
- 1 tsp vanilla extract
- A pinch of salt
- Optional: 1-2 tbsp unsweetened cocoa powder for chocolate variation

Baked Apple with Cinnamon and Walnuts

⏱ Time: 45 minutes	🍽 Serving Size: 4 servings
🥗 Prep Time: 15 minutes	👨‍🍳 Cook Time: 30 minutes

Ingredients:

- 4 medium-sized apples (such as Fuji or Honeycrisp)
- 1/4 cup chopped walnuts
- 1 tsp ground cinnamon
- 2 tbsp stevia or another diabetic-friendly sweetener

- 1/4 tsp ground nutmeg (optional)
- 1 tbsp unsalted butter, cut into 4 small pieces
- 1/2 cup water

Directions:

1. Set the oven's temperature to 175°C/350°F.

2. Core the apples, ensuring to remove seeds and creating a small well in the center, but not cutting through the bottom.

3. Chopped walnuts, cinnamon, sugar, and nutmeg (if used) should all be appropriately blended in a small basin.

4. Stuff each apple with the walnut mixture, pressing down slightly to ensure the filling is compact.

5. Place a small piece of butter on top of the filling for each apple.

6. Place the filled apples in an ovenproof tray. Pour water into the dish to help steam and soften the apples during baking.

7. Bake the apples for thirty minutes, or until soft, in a preheated oven. You can increase the bake time for softer apples.

8. Allow to cool for a few minutes, then serve warm. For an added touch, sprinkle with a dash of cinnamon before serving.

Nutrition Information:

Calories: 160, **Carbohydrates:** 26g, **Protein:** 2g, **Fat:** 7g, **Sugar:** 18g, **Sodium:** 2mg, **Fiber:** 5g.

Vegan Chocolate Chip Cookies (sugar-free)

Time: 25 minutes	Serving Size: 12 cookies
Prep Time: 10 minutes	Cook Time: 15 minutes

Ingredients:

- 1 cup almond flour
- 1/2 cup coconut flour
- 1/2 tsp baking soda
- 1/4 tsp salt
- 1/2 cup coconut oil, melted
- 1/4 cup unsweetened applesauce
- 1 tsp vanilla extract
- 1/2 cup sugar-free dark chocolate chips (like Lily's)
- 1/4 cup monk fruit sweetener or stevia
- Six tablespoons water and two tablespoons flaxseed meal (flax egg)

Directions:

1. Set the oven's temperature to 175°C/350°F. Line a baking sheet with parchment paper.

2. Mix almond flour, coconut flour, baking soda, and salt in a large mixing basin.

3. Melt the coconut oil, add the applesauce, vanilla essence, and monk fruit sweetener (or stevia) to a different bowl.

4. Mixing until just mixed, pour the wet mixture into the dry mixture.

5. Add the sugar-free chocolate chips and mix well.

6. Drop tablespoons of the dough, separated by about 2 inches, onto the baking sheet that has been prepared.

7. Using the back of a spoon, slightly flatten each cookie.

8. Bake in a preheated oven for 12 to 15 minutes, or until the sides begin to turn brown.

9. After a few minutes of cooling on the baking sheet, move the cookies to a wire rack to finish cooling.

Nutrition Information:

Calories: 152, **Carbohydrates:** 8g, **Protein:** 3g, **Fat:** 13g, **Sugar:** 1g, **Sodium:** 90mg, **Fiber:** 3g.

Nutrition Information:

Calories: 25, **Carbohydrates:** 7g, **Protein:** 0.5g, **Fat:** 0.2g, **Sugar:** 4g, **Sodium:** 2mg, **Fiber:** 2g.

Raspberry and Lemon Sorbet

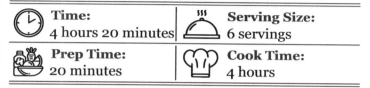

⏰ **Time:** 4 hours 20 minutes	🍽 **Serving Size:** 6 servings
🥗 **Prep Time:** 20 minutes	👨‍🍳 **Cook Time:** 4 hours

Ingredients:

- 2 cups fresh raspberries
- 1/2 cup of recently extracted lemon juice (about three lemons)
- 3/4 cup water
- 1/3 cup monk fruit sweetener or stevia (adjust according to desired sweetness)
- 1 tsp lemon zest

Directions:

1. Combine raspberries, lemon juice, water, and monk fruit sweetener (or stevia) in a blender. Blend until smooth.

2. Using a spatula to push out as much liquid as possible, strain the mixture through a fine-mesh sieve into a bowl. Discard the seeds.

3. Stir in the lemon zest.

4. After transferring the mixture to a shallow dish, freeze it for half an hour.

5. After 30 minutes, take it out and scrape with a fork to break any ice crystals forming on the surface. Repeat this scraping process every 30 minutes for about 3 hours.

6. Once the sorbet is set and smooth, let it rest in the freezer for another hour.

7. Before serving, allow the sorbet to sit at room temperature for 5-7 minutes to make scooping easier.

Pecan and Date Stuffed Pears

⏰ **Time:** 50 minutes	🍽 **Serving Size:** 4 servings
🥗 **Prep Time:** 20 minutes	👨‍🍳 **Cook Time:** 30 minutes

Ingredients:

- 4 medium-sized ripe pears
- 1/2 cup chopped pecans
- 1/2 cup finely chopped dates
- 1/4 teaspoon ground cinnamon
- 1/4 teaspoon ground nutmeg
- 1/2 teaspoon vanilla extract
- Zest of 1 orange
- 1 cup water
- 1 tablespoon lemon juice

Directions:

1. Set the oven temperature to 350°F (175°C).

2. Cut the tops off the pears and scoop out the core, creating a hollow space without breaking the pear. A melon baller works well for this.

3. Chopped pecans, dates, nutmeg, cinnamon, vanilla essence, and orange zest should all be appropriately blended in a medium-sized basin.

4. Carefully stuff each pear with the pecan and date mixture, pressing down to fill the hollow space.

5. In a baking dish, pour the water and lemon juice.

6. Place the stuffed pears into the baking dish,

ensuring they sit upright.

7. After preheating the oven, place aluminum foil over the dish and bake for about half an hour or until the pears are tender.

8. Please remove it from the oven and let it cool down a little before serving.

Nutrition Information:

Calories: 200, **Carbohydrates:** 42g, **Protein:** 2g, **Fat:** 6g, **Sugar:** 31g, **Sodium:** 2mg, **Fiber:** 7g.

Blueberry Almond Crumble (sugar-free)

🕐	**Time:** 45 minutes	🍽	**Serving Size:** 6 servings
🥗	**Prep Time:** 15 minutes	👨‍🍳	**Cook Time:** 30 minutes

Ingredients:

- 3 cups fresh blueberries
- 1 cup almond flour
- 1/2 cup chopped almonds
- 1/4 cup coconut oil, melted
- 1 tsp vanilla extract
- 1 tbsp ground chia

seeds (for binding)

- 1 tsp ground cinnamon
- Zest of 1 lemon
- 1/4 cup erythritol (natural sugar substitute)
- A pinch of salt

Directions:

1. Preheat the oven to 350°F (175°C).

2. In a mixing bowl, combine the blueberries with half of the erythritol, the lemon zest, and 1/2 tsp of cinnamon. Toss to coat well.

3. Transfer the blueberry mixture to a medium-sized baking dish.

4. Mix almond flour, chopped almonds, coconut oil, vanilla extract, chia seeds, the remaining erythritol, and cinnamon until it forms a crumbly texture.

5. Sprinkle the almond mixture evenly over the blueberries.

6. Place in the oven and bake for 30 minutes until the topping is golden brown and the blueberries are bubbly.

7. Allow to cool for a few minutes before serving. Best enjoyed warm.

Nutrition Information:

Calories: 250, **Carbohydrates:** 15g, **Protein:** 5g, **Fat:** 20g, **Sugar:** 5g, **Sodium:** 20mg, **Fiber:** 4g.

Mango and Lime Gelato

🕐	**Time:** 4 hours 15 minutes	🍽	**Serving Size:** 6 servings
🥗	**Prep Time:** 15 minutes	👨‍🍳	**Cook Time:** 4 hours

Ingredients:

- 3 ripe mangoes, peeled and pitted
- Juice and zest of 2 limes
- 1/3 cup erythritol (natural sugar

substitute)

- 1 cup full-fat coconut milk
- 1 tsp vanilla extract
- A pinch of salt

Directions:

1. Mango flesh, lime juice, zest, erythritol, coconut milk, vanilla extract, and salt should all be combined in a blender or food processor. Blend until the mixture is smooth.

2. Taste and adjust sweetness if needed.

3. Once the mixture has reached a creamy,

soft-serve consistency, transfer it to an ice cream machine and churn it according to the manufacturer's directions. If you don't have an ice cream maker, you may still use a shallow dish to hold the mixture in the freezer for around 4 hours, stirring every 30 minutes to break up any ice crystals.

4. Once churned, transfer the gelato to a lidded container and freeze for at least 2 hours to firm up.

5. Before serving, let it sit at room temperature for 5-10 minutes to soften slightly. Scoop into bowls or cones, and enjoy!

Nutrition Information:

Calories: 120, **Carbohydrates:** 28g, **Protein:** 1g, **Fat:** 5g, **Sugar:** 20g, **Sodium:** 10mg, **Fiber:** 3g.

bursts, stirring every 20 seconds, until it's smooth and fully melted.

3. Cover each strawberry about 3/4 of the way up after dipping it into the melted chocolate.

4. Sprinkle or roll the chocolate-covered portion of the strawberry in the crushed almonds.

5. Place the dipped strawberries on the prepared tray.

6. Once all strawberries are dipped and coated, place the tray in the refrigerator for about 30 minutes or until the chocolate has solidified.

7. When ready to eat, serve right away or put in the fridge.

Nutrition Information:

Calories: 80, **Carbohydrates:** 7g, **Protein:** 2g, **Fat:** 6g, **Sugar:** 2g, **Sodium:** 5mg, **Fiber:** 3g.

Chocolate Dipped Strawberries with Crushed Almonds

Time: 45 minutes	Serving Size: 12 strawberries
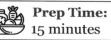 Prep Time: 15 minutes	Cook Time: 30 minutes

Ingredients:

- 12 large strawberries, washed and dried thoroughly
- 4 oz sugar-free dark chocolate
- 1/2 cup almonds, crushed
- 1 tsp coconut oil

Directions:

1. Place a piece of parchment paper on a tray or baking sheet.

2. In a microwave-safe bowl, combine the sugar-free dark chocolate and coconut oil. Heat the chocolate in the microwave for 20-second

Chapter 11: Refreshing and Nutritious Drinks

Green Detox Smoothie

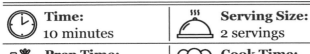

⏰ Time: 10 minutes	🍽 Serving Size: 2 servings
🥗 Prep Time: 10 minutes	👨‍🍳 Cook Time: 0 minutes

Ingredients:

- 1 cup kale, washed and de-stemmed
- 1 cup spinach, washed
- 1 small cucumber, sliced
- 1 green apple, cored and sliced
- 1 tablespoon chia seeds
- 1 tablespoon lemon juice
- 2 cups unsweetened almond milk
- A handful of ice cubes (optional)
- 1 tablespoon fresh ginger, grated (optional for added detoxifying effects and flavor)

Directions:

1. Combine kale, spinach, cucumber, green apple, chia seeds, lemon juice, ginger (if using), and almond milk in a blender.

2. Blend on high until all the ingredients are well combined, and the smoothie is smooth.

3. W thin out any excess mixture by adding water or almond milk to get the right consistency.

4. Pour into glasses and serve immediately.

Nutrition Information:

Calories: 190, **Carbohydrates:** 32g, **Protein:** 6g, **Fat:** 6g, **Sugar:** 14g, **Sodium:** 180mg, **Fiber:** 9g.

Iced Cinnamon Almond Milk Latte

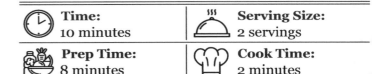

⏰ Time: 10 minutes	🍽 Serving Size: 2 servings
🥗 Prep Time: 8 minutes	👨‍🍳 Cook Time: 2 minutes

Ingredients:

- 2 cups unsweetened almond milk
- 2 espresso shots or a quarter-cup of strongly brewed, chilled coffee
- 1 teaspoon ground cinnamon
- 1 tablespoon sugar-free vanilla syrup (or adjust to taste)
- Ice cubes
- Cinnamon stick (for garnish, optional)

Directions:

1. Brew your espresso or coffee and allow it to cool.

2. Heat the almond milk over medium heat in a small saucepan. Do not bring it to a boil. Once it is warm, remove it from the heat.

3. Stir in the ground cinnamon and sugar-free vanilla syrup into the warm almond milk until well combined.

4. Fill two glasses with ice cubes.

5. Pour the cooled espresso or coffee over the ice in each glass.

6. Slowly pour the cinnamon almond milk mixture over the coffee.

7. If desired, stir gently and garnish with a cinnamon stick.

8. Serve immediately and enjoy!

Nutrition Information:

Calories: 60, **Carbohydrates:** 4g, **Protein:** 2g, **Fat:** 4g, **Sugar:** 0g, **Sodium:** 340mg, **Fiber:** 1g.

and water in a blender.

2. Process on high until creamy and smooth.

3. Add more water or almond milk to the shake if it's too thick for consistency.

4. For a colder shake, add ice cubes and blend again.

5. Once blended to your liking, taste and add vanilla extract if desired for added flavor.

6. After dividing the shake between two glasses, serve right away. Enjoy the nutrient-packed power shake!

Nutrition Information:

Calories: 310, **Carbohydrates:** 32g, **Protein:** 10g, **Fat:** 18g, **Sugar:** 10g, **Sodium:** 185mg, **Fiber:** 13g.

Blueberry and Spinach Power Shake

 Time: 10 minutes	Serving Size: 2 servings
Prep Time: 10 minutes	Cook Time: 0 minutes

Ingredients:

- 1 cup fresh blueberries (can also use frozen)
- 2 cups fresh spinach leaves, washed
- 1 cup unsweetened almond milk
- 1 tablespoon chia seeds
- 1/2 ripe avocado
- 1 tablespoon sugar-

free vanilla protein powder

- Add up to 1/2 cup of cold water to achieve the desired consistency.
- A handful of ice cubes (optional, especially if using frozen blueberries)
- 1 teaspoon sugar-free vanilla extract (optional for added flavor)

Directions:

1. Combine the blueberries, spinach, almond milk, chia seeds, avocado, protein powder,

Refreshing Cucumber and Mint Infusion

Time: 2 hours 5 minutes	Serving Size: 4 servings
Prep Time: 5 minutes	Cook Time: 2 hours

Ingredients:

- 1 large cucumber, thinly sliced
- 10-12 fresh mint leaves, washed and slightly bruised
- 4 cups (1 liter) of cold

water

- Ice cubes (optional)
- 1 tablespoon of recently extracted lemon juice (optional for a zesty kick)

Directions:

1. Combine sliced cucumber, mint leaves, and water in a large pitcher.

2. Add freshly squeezed lemon juice to give a subtle tangy flavor if desired.

3. Let the mixture steep in the refrigerator for at

least two hours or overnight for an even more intense flavor.

4. Before serving, give the infusion a gentle stir and pour into glasses. Add ice cubes if desired.

5. Enjoy the refreshing taste of cucumber and mint, perfect for a hot day!

Nutrition Information:

Calories: 30, **Carbohydrates:** 7g, **Protein:** 1g, **Fat:** 0g, **Sugar:** 3g, **Sodium:** 30mg, **Fiber:** 1g.

Mango and Turmeric Smoothie

⏰ **Time:** 10 minutes	🍲 **Serving Size:** 2 servings
🥗 **Prep Time:** 10 minutes	👨‍🍳 **Cook Time:** 0 minutes

Ingredients:

• 1 ripe mango, peeled, pitted, and chopped

• 1 cup unsweetened almond milk

• 1/2 teaspoon ground turmeric

• 1 tablespoon chia seeds

• 1/2 teaspoon vanilla extract

• A small amount of black pepper (to improve turmeric's ability to absorb curcumin)

• Ice cubes (optional)

• To taste, add stevia or monk fruit sweetener.

Directions:

1. Place chopped mango, almond milk, ground turmeric, chia seeds, vanilla extract, and black pepper into a blender.

2. Blend on high until smooth. To get the right consistency, thin any excess mixture with more almond milk.

3. Taste and add a natural sweetener like stevia or monk fruit, if desired, and blend again until well combined.

4. Pour into glasses, add ice cubes if you like, and enjoy your nutritious tropical treat!

Nutrition Information:

Calories: 220, **Carbohydrates:** 45g, **Protein:** 4g, **Fat:** 5g, **Sugar:** 38g, **Sodium:** 185mg, **Fiber:** 7g.

Ginger and Lemon Herbal Tea

⏰ **Time:** 15 minutes	🍲 **Serving Size:** 2 servings
🥗 **Prep Time:** 5 minutes	👨‍🍳 **Cook Time:** 10 minutes

Ingredients:

• 2 cups of water

• 1-inch fresh ginger root, thinly sliced

• Juice of 1 lemon

• Zest of 1/2 lemon

• To taste, add stevia or monk fruit sweetener.

• 2 herbal tea bags (e.g., chamomile, rooibos, or plain herbal tea)

Directions:

1. Heat some water in a pot.

2. Add thinly sliced ginger to the boiling water. Reduce the heat and let it simmer for about 5 minutes.

3. After simmering, remove from heat and add the herbal tea bags. Let steep for another 5 minutes.

4. After removing the tea bags, squeeze in the lemon zest and juice. Mix well.

5. Taste and add natural sweetener, if desired.

6. Pour into mugs, and serve warm.

Nutrition Information:

Calories: 10, **Carbohydrates:** 3g, **Protein:** 0.5g, **Fat:** 0g, **Sugar:** 1g, **Sodium:** 10mg, **Fiber:** 0.5g.

Pomegranate and Lime Spritzer

Time: 10 minutes	Serving Size: 2 servings
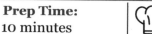 Prep Time: 10 minutes	Cook Time: 0 minutes

Ingredients:

- 1 cup freshly squeezed pomegranate juice (from about 2 medium pomegranates)
- Juice of 1 lime
- 2 cups sparkling water (unsweetened)
- Ice cubes
- Lime slices and pomegranate arils for garnish
- To taste, add stevia or monk fruit sweetener

Directions:

1. In a pitcher, combine the pomegranate juice and lime juice.

2. Taste and add a natural sweetener if desired.

3. Fill two glasses with ice cubes.

4. Pour the pomegranate and lime mixture into each glass, filling them halfway.

5. Top each glass with sparkling water and give a gentle stir.

6. Garnish with lime slices and pomegranate arils.

7. Serve immediately and enjoy!

Nutrition Information:

Calories: 140, **Carbohydrates:** 34g, **Protein:** 1g, **Fat:** 1g, **Sugar:** 30g, **Sodium:** 60mg, **Fiber:** 0.5g.

Raspberry and Chia Seed Lemonade

Time: 15 minutes	Serving Size: 4 servings
Prep Time: 10 minutes	Cook Time: 5 minutes

Ingredients:

- 1 cup fresh raspberries
- Juice of 4 large lemons
- 4 cups of water
- 2 tablespoons chia seeds
- To taste, add monk fruit or stevia sweetener.
- Fresh raspberries and lemon slices for garnish

Directions:

1. Puree the raspberries in a blender until they are smooth. Remove the seeds from the puree by straining them if you want a smoother texture.

2. Pour the water, lemon juice, and raspberry puree into a big pitcher.

3. Stir well.

4. Taste and add a natural sweetener if desired.

5. The chia seeds should swell, stir them in and let the mixture sit for around five minutes.

6. Chill the lemonade in the refrigerator for at least an hour.

7. Before serving, give the lemonade a good stir to redistribute the chia seeds.

8. Serve in glasses garnished with fresh raspberries and lemon slices.

Nutrition Information (for the whole recipe):

Calories: 150, **Carbohydrates:** 38g, **Protein:** 4g, **Fat:** 3g, **Sugar:** 12g, **Sodium:** 20mg, **Fiber:** 11g.

Coconut Water and Pineapple Hydrator

⏰ **Time:** 10 minutes	🍲 **Serving Size:** 4 servings
🥗 **Prep Time:** 10 minutes	👨‍🍳 **Cook Time:** 0 minutes

Ingredients:

- 3 cups coconut water
- 1 cup fresh pineapple chunks
- Juice of 1 lime
- A handful of fresh mint leaves
- 1 tablespoon chia seeds (optional for added nutrition)
- Ice cubes

Directions:

1. Put the pineapple chunks, lime juice, and half coconut water in a blender. Mix until homogeneous.
2. Pour the blended mixture into a pitcher.
3. Add the remaining coconut water to the pitcher.
4. If using, Add the chia seeds and let them sit until they swell, about 5 minutes.
5. Add ice cubes to glasses, and pour the hydrator over the ice.
6. Add a few mint leaves to the top of each serving.

Nutrition Information:

Calories: 240, **Carbohydrates:** 58g, **Protein:** 4g, **Fat:** 2g, **Sugar:** 44g, **Sodium:** 600mg, **Fiber:** 10g.

Ingredients:

- 2 cups unsweetened almond milk
- 1 scoop chocolate protein powder (low-carb, diabetic-friendly)
- 2 tablespoons almond butter
- 1 tablespoon unsweetened cocoa powder
- 1 tablespoon chia seeds
- A pinch of sea salt
- 1 teaspoon vanilla extract
- A handful of ice cubes

Directions:

1. Add the almond milk, chocolate protein powder, almond butter, unsweetened cocoa powder, chia seeds, sea salt, and vanilla extract in a blender.
2. Blend on high for about 1 minute or until the mixture is smooth.
3. Add the ice cubes and combine one more when the shake is excellent and foamy.
4. Pour into glasses and serve immediately.

Nutrition Information:

Calories: 420, **Carbohydrates:** 28g, **Protein:** 32g, **Fat:** 24g, **Sugar:** 4g, **Sodium:** 370mg, **Fiber:** 14g.

Chocolate and Almond Protein Shake

⏰ **Time:** 7 minutes	🍲 **Serving Size:** 2 servings
🥗 **Prep Time:** 5 minutes	👨‍🍳 **Cook Time:** 2 minutes

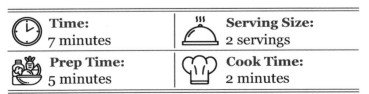

Chapter 12: 28-Day Meal Prep Plan

Day	Breakfast	Lunch	Dinner	Snack	Beverage
1	Almond Flour Pancakes with Blueberry Sauce	Grilled Chicken Salad with Balsamic Reduction	Vegan Lentil and Vegetable Curry	Stuffed Mini Bell Peppers	Ginger and Lemon Herbal Tea
2	Quinoa and Berry Morning Bowl	Lemon Herb Roasted Turkey Thighs	Spaghetti Squash with Tomato Basil Sauce	Spicy Roasted Chickpeas	Blueberry and Spinach Power Shake
3	Spinach and Feta Breakfast Scramble	Baked Chicken with Sun-dried Tomato Pesto	Herb-Crusted Salmon with Asparagus	Baked Spinach and Cheese Stuffed Mushrooms	Refreshing Cucumber and Mint Infusion
4	Diabetic-friendly Whole Grain Muffins	Mediterranean Chicken Wrap	Vegan Thai Green Curry with Veggies	Cauliflower Tots with Dipping Sauce	Pomegranate and Lime Spritzer
5	Chia Seed Pudding with Fresh Mango	Beef and Broccoli Stir Fry with Sesame Seeds	Tuna and Olive Pasta Salad	Sweet Potato and Rosemary Bites	Chocolate and Almond Protein Shake
6	Broccoli and Cheese Frittata	Pork Loin with Apple Cider Reduction	Spinach and Chickpea Coconut Curry	Tangy Tomato Bruschetta	Raspberry and Chia Seed Lemonade
7	Overnight Oats with Cinnamon and Apple	Herb-Crusted Lamb Chops	Stuffed Bell Peppers with Quinoa and Veggies	Asparagus Wrapped in Prosciutto	Mango and Turmeric Smoothie
8	High-Protein Breakfast Smoothie	Spiced Beef Kebabs	Eggplant and Tomato Casserole	Garlic Parmesan Green Bean Fries	Iced Cinnamon Almond Milk Latte
9	Avocado and Tomato Breakfast Bruschetta	Pork Tenderloin with Mushroom Gravy	Seared Scallops with Garlic Spinach	Baked Zucchini Fries	Coconut Water and Pineapple Hydrator
10	Multi-seed Granola with Unsweetened Yogurt	Lamb and Spinach Curry (low-fat version)	Vegan Tempeh Tacos	Cucumber and Avocado Rolls	Green Detox Smoothie
11	Vegetable-Stuffed Omelette	Grilled Pork Salad with Lime Dressing	Spinach and Mushroom Quiche (egg-free)	Stuffed Mini Bell Peppers	Refreshing Cucumber and Mint Infusion
12	Nutty Breakfast Bars	Beef Teriyaki with Steamed Veggies	Vegan Lentil and Vegetable Curry	Spicy Roasted Chickpeas	Ginger and Lemon Herbal Tea
13	Flaxseed and Raspberry Muffins	Mediterranean Chicken Wrap	Vegan Thai Green Curry with Veggies	Tangy Tomato Bruschetta	Blueberry and Spinach Power Shake
14	Sausage and Pepper Breakfast Casserole	Lamb Tagine with Apricots	Lobster Salad with Avocado and Greens	Sweet Potato and Rosemary Bites	Chocolate and Almond Protein Shake
15	Multi-seed Granola with Unsweetened Yogurt	Pork and Pineapple Skewers	Spinach and Chickpea Coconut Curry	Baked Zucchini Fries	Iced Cinnamon Almond Milk Latte
16	Overnight Oats with Cinnamon and Apple	Herb-Crusted Salmon with Asparagus	Roasted Vegetable and Farro Salad	Asparagus Wrapped in Prosciutto	Raspberry and Chia Seed Lemonade
17	High-Protein Breakfast Smoothie	Balsamic Glazed Pork Ribs	Vegan Lentil and Vegetable Curry	Garlic Parmesan Green Bean Fries	Pomegranate and Lime Spritzer
18	Avocado and Tomato Breakfast Bruschetta	Lemon Butter Grilled Shrimp	Chickpea and Kale Stir Fry	Stuffed Mini Bell Peppers	Coconut Water and Pineapple Hydrator

Day	Breakfast	Lunch	Dinner	Snack	Beverage
19	Chia Seed Pudding with Fresh Mango	Rosemary and Lemon Lamb Stir Fry	Spinach and Feta Breakfast Scramble (yes, breakfast for dinner!)	Tangy Tomato Bruschetta	Mango and Turmeric Smoothie
20	Broccoli and Cheese Frittata	Sizzling Beef and Pepper Fajitas	Quinoa and Roasted Veggie Bowl	Baked Spinach and Cheese Stuffed Mushrooms	Green Detox Smoothie
21	Diabetic-friendly Whole Grain Muffins	Lemon Herb Roasted Turkey Thighs	Eggplant and Tomato Casserole	Spicy Roasted Chickpeas	Blueberry and Spinach Power Shake
22	Quinoa and Berry Morning Bowl	Grilled Mackerel with Lemon Herb Dressing	Lentil and Spinach Stuffed Tomatoes	Tangy Tomato Bruschetta	Iced Cinnamon Almond Milk Latte
23	Spinach and Feta Breakfast Scramble	Chicken Spinach and Feta Stuffed Peppers	Spaghetti Squash with Tomato Basil Sauce	Cucumber and Avocado Rolls	Ginger and Lemon Herbal Tea
24	Overnight Oats with Cinnamon and Apple	Prawn and Zucchini Noodle Stir Fry	Vegan Tempeh Tacos	Asparagus Wrapped in Prosciutto	Chocolate and Almond Protein Shake
25	High-Protein Breakfast Smoothie	Beef and Vegetable Barley Soup	Vegan Tuscan White Bean Soup	Sweet Potato and Rosemary Bites	Raspberry and Chia Seed Lemonade
26	Broccoli and Cheese Frittata	Herb-Crusted Lamb Chops	Stuffed Bell Peppers with Quinoa and Veggies	Baked Spinach and Cheese Stuffed Mushrooms	Coconut Water and Pineapple Hydrator
27	Almond Flour Pancakes with Blueberry Sauce	Mediterranean Chicken Wrap	Barley and Mushroom Risotto	Baked Zucchini Fries	Pomegranate and Lime Spritzer
28	Multi-seed Granola with Unsweetened Yogurt	Rosemary Turkey Meatballs	Chickpea and Veggie Burger Patties	Cauliflower Tots with Dipping Sauce	Green Detox Smoothie

Conclusion outline

The diabetic diet, much more than a mere set of guidelines, represents a commitment to vibrant health, delicious foods, and balanced living. Rooted in evidence-based nutrition, this diet is not about sacrificing taste or feeling restricted. It's about understanding the power of nutritious foods, their direct impact on blood sugar, and their broader benefits to overall well-being.

In today's world, where instant gratification often eclipses long-term wellness, it becomes tempting to gravitate towards fad diets that promise swift results. Unfortunately, the modern dietary landscape is cluttered with refined sugars, trans fats, and heavily processed foods. These disrupt blood sugar levels and deprive our bodies of vital nutrients, potentially igniting numerous health ailments. This is where the diabetic diet shines its light. Centered on low-glycemic foods, healthy fats, lean proteins, and a rainbow of fruits and vegetables, it addresses the very core of diabetic management while ensuring a nourished, thriving body.

Embracing the diabetic diet is a choice to live a life where each meal becomes an opportunity to nourish the body, stabilize energy, and relish the myriad flavors nature offers. The rewards, ranging from better glucose control, reduced diabetes-related complications, and enhanced vitality, are profound and plentiful. Moreover, an unsung benefit is the mental peace derived from knowing each bite is aligned with health.

As you explore the recipes and insights within this book, it's pivotal to remember that the diabetic diet is about continuous growth and learning. It's not a pursuit of flawless execution but of consistent, informed choices. Over time, as you resonate with the principles of this diet, you'll witness not just a metamorphosis in your health metrics but a renewed passion for the art of cooking and eating.

Through this cookbook, our mission has been to equip you with a holistic toolkit for your diabetic culinary journey. Boasting diverse recipes and a structured four-week meal plan, we aspire to make your dietary transition both pleasurable and straightforward.

As this chapter concludes, remember this is merely the commencement of your culinary voyage. The diabetic diet, much like any enduring philosophy, is marked by its resilience and flexibility. So, as you progress, tweak, innovate, and, most crucially, savor every moment.

Before you embark on this gastronomic adventure, a sincere appeal: if this cookbook has enlightened your culinary path, enriched your daily meals, or even unveiled a newfound favorite recipe, we'd cherish your feedback. A review on [platform name] would mean the world to us. Your reflections will refine our future endeavors and aid fellow diabetics in navigating their culinary course.

Thank you for choosing a journey steeped in health, taste, and mindful eating, and wishing you many delightful meals and a flourishing, vibrant life ahead!

References

American Diabetes Association. (2022). Nutrition Therapy for Adults With Diabetes or Prediabetes: A Consensus Report. Diabetes Care, 45(5), 1-30.

Barnard, N. D., Cohen, J., Jenkins, D. J. A., Turner-McGrievy, G., Gloede, L., Green, A., & Ferdowsian, H. (2009). A low-fat vegan diet and a conventional diabetes diet in treating type 2 diabetes: a randomized, controlled, 74-wk clinical trial. American Journal of Clinical Nutrition, 89(5), 1588S-1596S.

Evert, A. B., & Franz, M. J. (2017). Evidence-based nutrition principles and recommendations for the treatment and prevention of diabetes. Diabetes Spectrum, 30(1), 61-74.

Franz, M. J., Boucher, J. L., Rutten-Ramos, S., & VanWormer, J. J. (2015). Lifestyle weight-loss intervention outcomes in overweight and obese adults with type 2 diabetes: a systematic review and meta-analysis of randomized clinical trials. Journal of the Academy of Nutrition and Dietetics, 115(9), 1447-1463.

Jenkins, D. J. A., Kendall, C. W. C., McKeown-Eyssen, G., Josse, R. G., Silverberg, J., Booth, G. L., ... & Singer, W. (2008). Effect of a low–glycemic index or a high–cereal fiber diet on type 2 diabetes. JAMA, 300(23), 2742-2753.

Mayer-Davis, E. J., Sparks, K. C., Hirst, K., Costacou, T., Lovejoy, J. C., Regensteiner, J. G., ... & Pi-Sunyer, X. (2004). Dietary intake in the diabetes prevention program cohort: baseline and 1-year post-randomization. Annals of Epidemiology, 14(10), 763-772.

Turner-McGrievy, G. M., Barnard, N. D., Cohen, J., Jenkins, D. J., Gloede, L., & Green, A. A. (2008). Changes in nutrient intake and dietary quality among participants with type 2 diabetes following a low-fat vegan or conventional diabetes diet for 22 weeks. Journal of the American Dietetic Association, 108(10), 1636-1645.

Warshaw, H., & Bolderman, K. (2004). Practical Carbohydrate Counting: A How-to-Teach Guide for Health Professionals. American Diabetes Association.

Wheeler, M. L., Dunbar, S. A., Jaacks, L. M., Karmally, W., Mayer-Davis, E. J., Wylie-Rosett, J., & Yancy, W. S. (2012). Macronutrients, food groups, and eating patterns in the management of diabetes. Diabetes Care, 35(2), 434-445.

The Diabetes Cookbook: 300 Recipes for Healthy Living (2017). Published by the American Diabetes Association.

Appendix 1: Measurement Conversion Chart

U.S. System	Metric
1 inch	2.54 centimeters
1 fluid ounce	29.57 milliliters
1 pint (16 ounces)	473.18 milliliters, 2 cups
1 quart (32 ounces)	1 liter, 4 cups
1 gallon (128 ounces)	4 liters, 16 cups
1 pound (16 ounces)	437.5 grams (0.4536 kilogram), 473.18 milliliters
1 ounces	2 tablespoons, 28 grams
1 cup (8 ounces)	237 milliliters
1 teaspoon	5 milliliters
1 tablespoon	15 milliliters (3 teaspoons)
Fahrenheit (subtract 32 and divide by 1.8 to get Celsius)	Centigrade (multiply by 1.8 and add 32 to get Fahrenheit)

Appendix 2: Index Recipes

A

B

This is an expanded index of primary ingredients and their corresponding recipes, filtered in alphabetical order.